I0014810

Hacked!

**A warning to all companies who use
IT and think
Cyber attacks happen to someone
else.**

By

Mike Lee & Brian Hitchen

First Edition

Copyright – Mike Lee & Brian Hitchen

All Rights Reserved

With the exception of Part 2, no part of this book may be reproduced in any form, by photocopying or by any electronic or mechanical means, including information storage or retrieval systems, without permission in writing from both the copyright owner and the publisher of this book

For Part 2 – The use of Part 2, is covered by the Open Government Licence
(www.nationalarchives.gov.uk/information-management/uk-gov-licensing-framework.htm).

Mike Lee & Brian Hitchen
2016

Hacked!

Able Smith & Winston found themselves the victim of an organised hack from a Russian based team. They were in the position of having insecure IT systems because of the way they designed and ran their internet presence.

We, the users, are under constant pressure to deliver and use the latest developments in IT, but for what benefit? Certainly not the business that finances those systems, nor the users or customers. The only people that benefit are the IT Vendors and technicians who ensure that we are constantly riding on an Upgrade Escalator while failing to understand the basics of IT and Information Security.

Read on and discover how this situation can affect and even ruin businesses, and how to break out of the cycle.

About the Authors

Mike Lee

Mike started his career in information technology when computers filled a large room but had the power of your sim card. Security was the lock on the computer room.

He held a number of jobs to do with operating, programming, managing, fixing and selling all types of computer. He now works for the UK government ensuring that UK-plc and the computers it uses are secure and resilient.

Mike is married with many children and grandchildren. He lives happily in West Sussex with his gorgeous wife Angie and in his spare time plays with cars, bikes, cycles, all types of new technology, and of course - computers.

Brian Hitchen

Brian worked in IT from 1970 until 2014. He spent the last 30 years working as IT Security Manager for a number of financial services organisations. In 1995 he installed the Cyber Forensics facilities as part of his security role. Since then he has investigated and prosecuted several high value financial crimes.

In 2014 he retired from full-time work and has since been researching Cyber Crime and the impact that it has on small to medium businesses, writing books, working as a STEM Ambassador, helping the South East Cyber Security Cluster, volunteering with the National Coast Watch as well as fundraising for his local Lifeboat.

Brian lives on the South Coast with his wife Linda.

Dedications

Mike Lee
This book is dedicated to Angie Johnson who gave constant encouragement and proof read many parts.

Then I would like to thank all of the bad managers, supervisors and directors that I have worked with who have shown me by example how not to deliver IT systems. Bless you guys – you know who you are!

Brian Hitchen
Thanks to Linda for the constant encouragement cups of tea and, most of all, for believing.

Thanks also to Leonard White, who was an Actor, Producer and Director. Some may remember The Avengers. Leonard was the Director of the original series and was the first person to put a woman at the heart of a TV series with a distinct role and a strong character. He gave valuable advice when I was writing my first book. In February 2016 he passed away at the age of 99. He was a good and valued friend to more people than he ever realised.

I also want to thank my parents, especially my late dad who taught me that no matter how little you know, there is always a manager in the company who knows less.

Cover Design
Many thanks to Linda Hitchen who designed the cover for the Small Business Assistance series, of which this is the second book.

Other Books
Disaster Avoidance by Brian Hitchen, Gary Hawkins and Paul Rumsey
Information Trickery by Mike Lee and Brian Hitchen – Now out of print
Cyberwall by Brian Hitchen and Paul Sawyer – Now out of print

Prologue

The following is a work of fiction. As its base it uses real events that have happened to companies in the recent past.

As such it is told as a narrative of how real people made mistakes in their business and suffered the consequences and it invites the reader to learn from those mistakes.

Real life is not like fiction; people don't necessarily live happily ever after. They continue to struggle on against near overwhelming odds. Life is hard work, business life even more so. The world is full of people trying to destroy or steal the ideas, information and business collateral that you have spent so much time and effort building. It is up to you to protect these assets and to continue making a living.

You will encounter many people trying to persuade you to spend money on things you don't need. There are also people trying to sell you things that will really benefit your business. The real expertise is being able to tell which is which and distinguish between the nice-to-have and the must-have.

In the area of Information Technology there are new inventions and methods which, when used correctly, will really benefit your company and the people working in it. There are other things, however that you absolutely don't need and can present you even more problems. In this book we give specific examples of companies that use older technology to great effect and their investment in that technology is rewarded. We also give examples of how other companies have successfully utilised new technology to give a business edge. Both are approaches are valid and the message we want to give is CHOOSE THE RIGHT TOOL FOR THE JOB AND UNDERSTAND THE RISKS AND BENEFITS.

The Internet is a fantastic opportunity that allows small to medium companies to have a global market-place and to benefit from low cost advertising and presence. However, there is pressure to speed up aspects of your business, but, you must be aware of the threats that exist to your business when trying to integrate new technologies and methods.

Please remember the above as you read this book. It IS fiction BUT it is fiction that you can learn from.

We hope you enjoy it.

How to read this book

The book is written in three parts. Part 1 deals with the main story and shows how a successful company found that they were vulnerable to a criminal attack that would eventually lead to their downfall. In part 2 we look at the UK Government Cyber Security Advice (10 steps to cyber security) and show how the company had failed to take this free adv ice and where they had failed. We also look at the consequences of their failures so we can see that the company is steadily becoming a greater target for the criminals. Part 3 gives some companies and organisations that you can go to for help. This is not meant to me a comprehensive list but rather some companies and organisations that we have dealt with in the past. We do not recommend these entities but offer them as a guide.

Part 1
The Story

Chapter 1

Steve Jones was feeling good and rightly so. It was April 2nd and he had achieved three things. First he had got right through yesterday without falling for any of the childish pranks of his fellow workers, pranks that they seemed to be really proud of. Pranks that they bragged about afterwards. He had seen the lot, he had noticed that the sugar was finer than normal and guessed correctly that it was salt. He had realised that the "system alert" could actually be a series of simple display messages that some clown had buried in their application program to fool the unwary.

The second thing he was proud of was the fact that he was about to leave work early to collect his new Mercedes, his new silver two-seater Mercedes.

And the third thing? That was what his Mercedes gave him. The feeling that he had finally arrived and made it in the dual world of advertising and IT and he was about to collect his Prize.

This was a new car, not just "new to him" A brand new car with the latest registration plate, no previous owners and a price tag that meant the insurance company had insisted on every security measure you could think of short of an armed guard.

Steve worked for Able Smith and Winston (ASW as it was more popularly known in the corporate world), a small but well established advertising agency in the City of London. The company had been around for years but had always remained one of the elite and well respected agencies. It had around 28 staff and 5 Directors and 2 interns. Sebastian Winston, the Managing Director of the company had been the founder of the original company, and it had grown steadily in size and value.
Steve was in charge of the computer network and the Internet system that were their window on the world. The web-site had been a massive success and Steve was proud of his baby and the rewards that it had brought. In just three years with the agency he had been promoted twice and his salary had gone through the roof. He was 28 years old with an impressive physique that had been earned in the nearby gym. He was enjoying life and took his work seriously, which was just as well as he was in charge of the network, the servers and the web-site. Steve was a generalist, he couldn't design an

encryption system but he could implement an encryption package. He wouldn't attempt to design a complete network but he could build and maintain a network that the suppliers had designed.

In short Steve was just what a small but rapidly growing company needed. He wasn't indispensable, you understand. If he were to walk under a bus the company wouldn't fold. We know this because his death **didn't** cause the company to collapse. Technology for technology's sake was what killed Steve and ultimately caused the demise of the company.

His was a responsible job but one that he knew he could handle. The IT Department consisted of him, Anne a 32 year old Technical Analyst, a number of network, database and systems support staff mainly in their early 20s, straight from university, and Paul Taylor, the IT Director.

Anne had much more experience than Steve, who was working at his second proper site since leaving University. His first job had been in a large IT department with a multi-national oil company. He hadn't felt that what he did really mattered so he had looked for a smaller team where he would be able to stand out. He had a good all round IT education and was familiar with the requirements of an Internet site. He made sure things ran smoothly and fast. It was less than six months since they had upgraded to their new servers and the implementation had been a dream.

He prided himself in working 'smart', doing the things that needed doing and not worrying about the irrelevant procedures that seemed to be there to hinder progress. Some companies were so tied up in red-tape that they could never hope to be ahead of the opposition, that was what it had been like in his first job, but this was different. He had a free hand to do what needed to be done and use his judgement for the rest. For example, the security of the network has to be dictated by the risk to the business, but Steve and Paul felt that they were able to make that decision in isolation from the business. Everyone knew that hackers went after the large companies where they had masses of personal data that could be copied and sold to criminals, ASW simply wasn't in that league, so the IT security had a lower priority and could wait.

Steve felt that the way the ASW network was designed was really clever. The accounting and HR systems were run on a separate small network that was not on the main office network. All staff and client data and all of the accounting information was protected from prying eyes. This had been a selling point of the new system. No-one can hack a computer that is not connected to a network. Paul, as IT Director was proud of the design of the systems and he had assured the rest of the Board that the company would be safe from attack. The board didn't understand computers but they could see the benefit of a really slick web-site and embracing the features of the Internet. They were also very appreciative of features such as e-mail, Skype and messaging applications that meant they were able to connect and talk to clients face to face without having to travel to their office.

Steve knew that hackers may be able to get in to their system but there would be nothing of interest if they did. It simply was not a risk. The accounting system was where the client list was held, where the invoices were processed. They didn't accept credit-cards on the web-site, in fact they didn't trade on the web. Steve and Paul had discussed many times that you adopted a simple "brochure" approach to the company web-site then the hackers would have no interest in it. Of course there were the vandals, kids really who would deface a web-site just for laughs, but he had a good Intrusion Detection System (IDS) that would warn him of an attack and take the appropriate action. In any case, all of the system files were backed up every day to a Cloud supplier so even if they managed to deface the system, he would have the original web-site back in operation within an hour or so.

He would eventually assess the vulnerability of their site and harden the operating system, it would be useful experience and it would look good on his CV but it simply was not a priority. He was far too busy to waste time on Cyber defence and even if he wanted to act, the business justification would be an uphill struggle and the board would always want to spend the money on new PCs, iPads and phones.

His mind drifted to his new Mercedes. Unlike the web-site, his car **was** a target and it had top of the range security, alarm, immobiliser, multi point cameras and a best of breed satellite tracking system. Computing was the same. Analyse the risk and take appropriate measures. He had done a course on risk analysis at University and he knew the basic principles. He also felt that 'Security Consultants' were simply there to generate fear and revenue. They would always overstate the risks.

Paul, the IT Director had said the same. He was a good guy, even if, at 42, he was probably past it. The best thing about Paul was that he understood what IT could do for the company. Paul felt that he was surrounded by so many negative managers in other jobs that it was amazing that they hadn't worn him down. Of course he understood the risks that they faced. He had been away on a number of courses and seminars that had dealt with computer security. All the business had to do was to take the orders. IT gave them the web-site to sell the goods as well as the tools to process and deliver what the customer wanted.

The last audit report had said they needed to improve the security of the installation, so they had agreed to a thorough review to keep the auditors at bay. But like Steve, Paul had more important things to do. Auditors - what did they know about the real world? Most of them were just middle aged suits from the City who thought they knew what it was like at the sharp end of business. They didn't have a clue. If ASW took every bit of advice the experts gave they would have to double the IT budget. Paul and Steve were proud of their IT Team. The web-site wasn't designed to be an online shop it was a brochure and a damn good one at that.

Steve checked the time for the tenth time that hour, it would soon be time to leave and collect his new car. He called Anne; she would cover for him while he was out of the office. She knew the systems and could react to an alert if the IDS system detected anything of interest. She was good. She was older than him and she had left one of the main high street Banks to make some serious money. She had worked at a number of the Internet sites during the boom years and had done very well. Then when the bubble burst, she had looked around for a small but safe company to work for. ASW was just upgrading their early Web-Site and seemed to be in an industry that would benefit from better use of technology, so she had applied for a job and had been taken on. She looked after all of their applications, like the accounts and the payroll system. She was OK, she had plenty of experience and she would keep an eye open for any problems.

ASW was a fairly small advertising agency but they had a number of good clients, profitable clients. The company had been going for years but had relied too much on a small number of loyal clients. Clients that had been gained through the personal contact of Sebastian Winston and the last remaining survivor of the original trio who had formed the company over 30 years before. Sebastian, or Seb as the rest of the directors referred to him, had relied on his school contacts for business. People he knew from his Public School days and who had obviously been influential in a number of companies and he seemed to have an incredible knack for sniffing out a business opportunity.

Business wasn't done like that now, at least a growing number of businesses weren't run that way. There were far more talented young men and women forcing their way to the top, not prepared to wait for promotions that were measured on a geological clock. These people took risks, lived hard and he admired them. Steve wanted ASW to be the same, to be far more dynamic. He liked the fact that ASW got things done and he was also pleased that they were always working on the latest technology or product. He also liked the fact that the ASW web-site was slick, attractive and fast, and he was proud that the IT department was small and dynamic. Under the direction of Paul, IT was starting to make a difference. They were beginning to move ahead of the opposition's use of technology and even though their rivals were envious, there was nothing they could do about it. Leading edge IT was the real power-house behind ASW, they were the new professionals and they would soon be seen as such. And even if it didn't work out, he had nothing to lose. Steve was young, getting noticed and he had a great future so he always made sure that his CV was up to date and as impressive as possible.

Steve saw himself as a solver of problems, a provider of opportunity for the company. When, some five months ago, he had overheard the head of advertising complaining that they couldn't get a courier for an urgent storyboard media clip on a CD he needed to send to Oxford, Steve had jumped in. He told the young executive that he could use his e-mail system to do the job in a fraction of the time and at no real cost. Steve had shown him how to use PGP so the file was encrypted and could safely be added as an attachment to an e-mail. All the executive would have to do was to phone the client and tell them the password to unlock the attachment. He was tempted to say that the attachment should be stored on the main server but then it

14

would be his problem to manage the space. If the attachments were stored on the PC of the ASW user, then "IT" wouldn't be responsible for the security of the clip. Of course, it also meant that the work wouldn't be backed up but these were trial files that would only be needed for a few weeks until the main advertising campaign started so there was a limit to the number that anyone would need to store. The exec duly did this and successfully delivered the video sample to the customer, who approved it that day.

Steve had felt good at the compliments he had been paid and Paul had been pleased that IT had solved a problem and saved the day. The Ad people realised that they could get storyboard and even video clips delivered much faster to their suppliers and the clients would benefit from the improved service.

Steve looked out of the window, it was a sunny afternoon and the City seemed a little less grey. It was busy with people rushing to meetings, doing deals, making money. Increasingly the UK was moving ahead of the opposition, it was making better use of IT than many of its competitor countries. In his opinion it was a good place to be and the more that IT drove business the better things would be for the people working in the computer industry. Companies were no longer using IT to provide them with information for the 'real work'. IT was becoming the core business of many companies. A growing number of them made their money out of their IT systems and quite a few of them didn't even realise it. Steve knew that he needed to look after "number one". He needed to make sure that he was learning the latest techniques. He would serve the company well and do a good job but only so long as it suited his personal ambition. Only so long as he was able to keep really up to date from a technical point of view.

Steve glanced at his watch again and realised that it was time to leave. As he put his coat on, he glanced again at the IDS monitor, nothing to report, no alerts, that was good he thought as he made for the door. What he didn't realise was the fact that the IDS was unlikely to issue any alerts. For the past three days, the threshold had been changed to the point where the only event that the IDS would report would be a full-scale Distributed Denial of Service (DDoS) attack.

The IDS would not notice a hacker or a small group of hackers working on their systems. The fact that there were three hackers currently inside their systems proved the point. They had been logged on for over four hours and they would be on the systems for at least another six. They had a great deal of data to copy. They had spent hours and hours locating all of the files that they wanted to duplicate and they were now helping themselves to the data. Anne wouldn't see anything, as the only thing to notice was the fact that the e-mail server was busy. A more specialist technician may have wondered why the network was running at the speed it was but he wasn't there to notice. For the past few days he had been distracted with far more important things, like his brand new silver Mercedes with its top of the range security.

Steve wasn't the only one to be distracted on that day. June was the HR Director, in fact she was the HR Department but she was well organised and competent at her job. For the most part she liked her work and the fact that she lived less than 2 miles from the office meant that she would walk to work unless the weather was really bad. At 42 and contentedly single after a brief but turbulent marriage that had ended ten years earlier, the job suited her lifestyle. The truth was that she was comfortably off. She had bought her third-floor two-bedroom flat at a time when the prices were more realistic than they were today and she could afford to buy nice clothes, which she really had an eye for. At 5 feet 6 inches tall and wearing size 12 clothes she could still turn heads, though not of the younger men. Still she was content with her lot in life and for the most part did a job, which she was good at, and enjoyed.

Today, however, she was not enjoying it and hadn't been for the past three weeks. She had been asked to look through the staff list and come up with some possible redundancies. She had been told that this was a high priority task by Sebastian, the Managing Director and she had needed to talk to the other Directors to see if they could suggest possible staff cuts. She had gone to see Malcolm Shoreham, the Finance Director and she was a little embarrassed to realise that it was the first time she had seen him alone since the Party last Friday

June had at times found Malcolm attractive but hadn't done anything about it. After all, she was living comfortably enough in her flat and while she occasionally missed the company of another person, well man actually, she was hardly pining for love. Last Friday they had both attended an after work drinks party given by Seb to celebrate his secretaries' birthday. June had made a little more effort than usual on her appearance and found an excuse to talk in private to him. She knew he was the same age as her and single but she really didn't know much about him. She knew that he was sometimes a secretive and difficult man to deal with at work and was not very popular, but she had put that own to him being the Financial Wizard and a bit of a nerd. When he did speak it was to comment on the state of the stock market or the effect that the government economic policy was having on "the markets". But for the most part he kept to himself and most people saw that as him being aloof.

Now she would … well, not make a play, exactly but she would see if there was any common ground. Yet after about five minutes of chatting and giving him her full attention she had begun to feel uncomfortable. It was clear that Malcolm felt ill at ease with her and was slightly embarrassed. The more she talked to him, the more she realised that she wasn't getting his attention. Twice she caught him looking for too long to the side of her shoulder at the people behind her. She had carefully looked round but all she could see were three of the IT guys joking with one of the prettier secretaries and the door to his office. Still it made her feel foolish and she was sure that Malcolm had been waiting for her to go so that he could wander over to the object of his attention. When she did move away, she was surprised to see him walk over to his office and go inside. She realised that she had been avoiding him ever since.

Now that she had to see him, she felt embarrassed, as if they had been having a secret affair and been caught out. This was stupid, she was a grown woman, happily divorced and he was a single man. There had been nothing between them and the chances were that Malcolm had not even noticed her 'move' at the party.

As it turned out, Malcolm was his usual business-like self. He was more concerned with the numbers that Sebastian had asked her to look at cutting. As Finance Director, he was acutely aware of the financial problems they faced but he was also sure that it was a short-term issue. They had some good prospects on the horizon and they only needed one of them to come good and they would be OK. However, Sebastian had been determined to look at all options and so he had agreed that June look at the staff numbers. He had told her to look at a possible re-structure with the loss of 5 jobs. She had spoken to the other directors and got them to send her their suggestions.

They all knew that the company had been suffering from a down-turn at some of its larger clients and found that its revenues had been falling. At the last Board Meeting, Roland Carter, ASW's Creative Director had suggested the idea of a merger with its biggest rival. The problem was that the larger company had less talented staff, poor offices and an aggressive attitude that, while successful would be a complete culture shock for the staff of ASW and their clients, who liked the way that ASW treated them with respect. It seemed that they were more interested in a long-term relationship than in squeezing out every last penny. If a merger was to be avoided, then ASW would have to reduce its overheads and it therefore fell to June to look at the staff numbers with as much input from the other directors as possible. This was one aspect of her job that she really hated and, as she sat at her desk looking at the list in front of her, she could only see people, not numbers or statistics. Now, in front of Malcolm, it all seemed so clinical, callous, somehow. She really hoped they could avoid the need to cut staff numbers.

Chapter 2

In Moscow the three young men hacking into the systems of ASW had no such distractions. They were completely focused and had been, on and off, for the past three weeks. This was not some school-boy prank. This was not a case of breaking the web-site and changing the wording or replacing a company graphic with a pornographic picture – a web-site defacement. This was a professional attack, well planned and paid for.

Towards the end of February a meeting had taken place in London. Present at the meeting were two people. Simon, a private 'security consultant' and 'Crazy Einstein' a Russian hacker who had accepted the academic challenge of a large cash payment to 'provide inside information on ASW'. Crazy Einstein looked the way that Hollywood would have depicted him. He was in his late teens, maybe a little older, painfully thin and with thick glasses and a goatee that was a minimum of 30 years out of date in the West. Crazy Einstein worked with four friends in a team called OBSKURE). This was an organisation that only really existed in Cyber space, or only on the Dark Net to be accurate. They offered their services as "security consultants" and were skilled at what they did and OBSKURE was more of a concept than a consultancy. They offered their services and depending on the job, a number of different "consultants" would come together to attack the. When they were working on a project they made use of an office that Crazy Einstein rented. It had very good facilities, fast internet and a never ending supply of Pizza and Coke (the drink). They were good at their trade and Simon had used them before for other clients. Being in Russia meant that there was almost no chance of them getting arrested for hacking into small European companies and this is what they specialised in, at least that is what they got paid for.

OBSKURE had their own web-site and they claimed, **"Our group OBSKURE specializes in security technology. We are always doing research into vulnerabilities in the main operating systems and application software, generally looking for bugs that we can either exploit or pass on to the software owners in return for rewards. OBSKURE was founded in 1996. We have experts in:**

Most programming languages
Network design and all Firewall makes

Encryption (both commercial and military)
Microsoft (all variants of their OS), Linux, Unix, Android (most variants), Apple (all variants of their OS)

The members that Crazy Einstein used came mainly from young, well educated men and women. Hacking teams of this type had started as teenagers who simply hacked for fun or to cause a bit of mischief but they could make serious money if they cracked the security of a target company. Each member of the team would only need to work for a few weeks a year and the rest of their time was free for them to write legitimate apps or research further into their specialisation.

Simon and Crazy Einstein sat in the back of the Macdonald's restaurant. No-one could overhear their conversation and Simon sipped at his coffee as he outlined what he wanted.

"I am after any company, client or staff information that you can get from Able Smith and Winston, you may have heard of them as ASW."

"The advertising agency?" Asked Crazy Einstein who was well up on who did what in London and New York.

"Yes." Simon stated flatly as he pushed an envelope containing $2,000 across the table. The arrangements were the same as always, the cash was for incidental expenses but the bulk of the fee would be paid in Bitcoins that were virtually untraceable. Crazy Einstein would arrange the hack and if they obtained useful information Simon would pay them depending on the value of the information to his client. He finished his coffee and left Crazy Einstein to his Big Mac and Fries. He knew he would hear nothing for a few weeks but he could wait.

They had chatted about the target and Simon gave him a few pointers and the sort of information that 'his client' was after. There had to be a degree of trust between Simon and Crazy Einstein, after all they had worked together before and would no-doubt work together again. It was a mutually beneficial arrangement. Industrial espionage was highly profitable. In a take-over, it could save the 'client company' millions of pounds for an outlay of a few thousand if they knew the true value of the company, not just the figures that were published after being manipulated by the accountants. If they were lucky, they could often find information that would let them put pressure on a Director, information that he or she would be keen to keep away from the Regulators, their fellow Directors, a partner or even the Police. Simon had a reputation for delivering the goods. He had been recommended for the job and would earn his seemingly exorbitant fee.

Crazy Einstein didn't own OBSKURE, in theory no-one did, it was supposed to be run as a collective. In reality, OBSKURE was owned by it's founder, aLph4Num3ric (alphanumeric). He was older than the rest of the team, late 40's and he was well known in hacker circles. His early exploits had earned him a reputation as a Unix expert and he had penetrated some of the more sensitive military networks. That was in the days when the military didn't understand the risks that computer networks posed and there were far too many holes in them. The fact remains that aLph4Num3ric didn't care to venture outside Russia for fear of arrest. He preferred to let the younger members of the firm do the travelling. They loved it of course, it made them feel like James Bond.

With the job accepted and the target known, Crazy Einstein would return to Moscow and they could then plan how to attack the site. They knew that the key to their success was not to let the target know they were under attack and for many companies that was not so easy. They would have to see how good the ASW Security was. They would also have to schedule the work. It seemed that there would soon be a flood of take-overs in London and New York judging by the number of companies that they had been asked to target.

Crazy Einstein looked at his watch, he had given Simon a five-minute start and he rose from the table and left the restaurant, turning left to stroll through the streets of the City. He had walked, ambled really, about half a mile when he passed the doors of an expensive health club. He missed seeing Steve Jones by a matter of seconds. Their eyes never met and neither was even aware of the other. Steve came out of the gym and walked up the road, about ten yards behind Crazy Einstein. In a city of strangers one more didn't attract Steve's attention. It was probably just as well. Crazy Einstein was a sensitive young man and he would have coped badly had he met the man who's death would be caused as a result of OBSKURE taking this particular contract.

Chapter 3

It was the middle of April, one of those extra warm, clear days that convinces you that Summer is almost here, just before the weather turns and reminds you that this is England and nothing, weather-wise can be taken for granted. The day was warm though and Paul felt some slight optimism. ASW had just heard that MAZOTA, the second biggest Car Manufacturer in Japan had been pleased with the outline for their new UK ad campaign. There was a good chance that this would lead to a series of adverts and everyone at ASW was feeling really pleased. They had beaten some stiff opposition for the original advert and the client seemed to be impressed with the outline. Now they were ready to deliver the completed Video Clips.

There was one 30 second "full" version and three 15 second extracts that would form the bulk of the campaign. They all had the same 'strap-line', the words "The drive in your life" that would be the basis of the entire campaign. It was hoped that within two months, 75-80% of their target audience would be using the strap-line in everyday speech. It was brilliant and simple. The sign of pure genius. Simple or brilliant alone were not enough, it had to be both. The guys from MAZOTA UK were particularly pleased with it as they had been working hard to get the car launched ahead of the new LEXDA model that was due out this year and there was furious rivalry between them

Paul was feeling pleased that the company would be able to turn the corner in its fortunes and he and his staff would be secure once again. He was struck with a general feeling of optimism that things were getting better. The company's fortunes seemed to be improving. With luck the threat of redundancies would soon be lifted. If that happened, then he would be free to think seriously about Alyson. He had been having an affair with her for the best part of two years and the strain of living a double life was beginning to tell. He was sure his wife had begun to suspect and he had been snappy at work. He had to get a grip or he would be out of a job. He knew he had taken some really stupid risks, like booking himself into seminars or training courses and then skipping most of them so that he could be with Alyson. For a while he had feared that she would be made redundant and he couldn't really break up with her if she were about to find herself out of work. It would look too callous, oh, forget what it "looked like", it would BE too callous. Now, however, things were on the up and he felt great.

He felt like that for about seven minutes until his PC had booted up and he opened his e-mail to start the familiar routine of another working day. Within seconds he was staring fixedly at the screen, his fingers curled idly round the mouse, as he read and re-read a message that made no sense to him. Gradually he moved from blank incomprehension to a dawning sense of disaster and the colour drained from his face. - The item was a return receipt in his e-mail in-box. He stared in total disbelief. He was looking at a system generated message but one that he should never have seen.

Two weeks earlier he had sent an e-mail to June, the HR Director explaining which of his staff he could afford to lose. He had been so careful to send the message with a return receipt so that he would know when she had received it, or rather when she had opened the message. Then he had deleted the original e-mail so that no-one would be able to see what he had written. Now, in front of him was a return-receipt that told him the message had been read by June at 06:00 that morning. There were two problems, the first of which was that June had read the e-mail the day he sent it and he had already had a return receipt from her. No matter how many times she read it again, the system would not issue another receipt. It had to be another user. That meant that someone with read access to her e-mail had read it. Other than June herself, the only people in the company who could read her e-mails were himself and Steve, no one else had Admin authority. June had not given anyone else read access to her e-mails and he and Steve were the only people with Admin rights to the e-mail system. The second problem was even worse. He knew for a fact that no-one had been in the office at 06:00, in fact he had been the first to arrive just before 08:00 that morning.

He quickly checked the system logs to see if anyone was logged on to the systems, it was possible that one of the Directors had connected in remotely. Maybe June had given them read access to her e-mails without him knowing. He looked through the logs and started to feel sick! He saw that Joseph had logged on to the system at 01:00 that morning. Now he became really worried. Apart from the apparent dedication of Joseph, he knew that there wasn't a Joseph working for ASW. He had never defined a user of that name to the system.

He looked at the log for at least two minutes before it struck him. Steve was the only other person who could have put the account on the system. If he hadn't defined Joseph, then they had an unauthorised user on the system. He called Steve into his office, the tone of the summons giving too much away. Steve raced in and saw the worried face of Paul still staring at his screen. Paul seemed somehow lost in his large executive office. Sat behind his L-shaped desk he would normally fill the room, now he seemed to be a small part of it. Steve looked around at the large circular meeting table that could comfortably seat six. He looked at the two visitors chairs in front of Paul's desk. He looked at the large display cabinet that housed the drinks cupboard and the TV systems. Everything was 'normal' yet Paul seemed to be lost in his own office.

"There's an e-mail account in the name of Joseph." Paul said without looking up from the screen. "What can you tell me about it?"

"Joseph? Nothing, I haven't defined anyone by that name." Steve said.

Paul looked up and made eye contact with Steve, then asked in a steady voice. "Are you absolutely sure?"

"Yeah, positive. I know all of the accounts that we have on the system and he isn't one of them."

"Well he is now and he seems to have read access to June's e-mails." Said Paul in a deliberately slow flat voice. "Have you given anyone Admin authority on the system?"

"Absolutely not! I don't trust anyone else enough to give them that level of authority." Paul believed him on that one. Steve continued. "When was this Joseph defined?"

Paul looked at him and felt stupid, he should have checked that as one of the first things he had done. He entered a few commands and looked at Steve with real horror in his eyes.

"He was defined a few weeks earlier." The voice was almost a whisper as he continued. "At oh two hundred on March the 25th and my userid was used to define Joseph giving him admin rights on the system."

Paul looked at Steve and said in slow, measured tones.

"You realise what this means? We have been hacked."

"In fact we were hacked just over three weeks ago." They looked at each other in shared disbelief. This was the one thing that they were both sure couldn't happen. They knew they had no accounts data or customer details on-line and no-matter what a hacker did they couldn't get money out of the systems. What would a hacker gain from getting into their system? He looked at Steve and realised that he needed him to help trace what the hackers had been doing but he couldn't let him look at the e-mails. It was clear that June still had his e-mail about possible redundancies and she would almost certainly have others. In addition, most of the other managers wouldn't have been as careful as him with their e-mails. There would probably be a number of 'sensitive' e-mails on the system. With a feeling of real dread he realised that the hacker would almost certainly have read most of the e-mails on the system. After all they were a small shop and it wouldn't take long to read all of the internal stuff. In fact it was probably the size of the systems that had trapped the hacker. It was almost unheard of for anyone in ASW to use a return receipt for an e-mail, most of the e-mails were confirming conversations, or reminders. The sort of thing that people would have sent a memo about a few years before. It was only because Paul was worried about the content of his e-mail to June that he had used the return receipt facility. The chances were that the hacker had been careful not to trigger any receipts in the early days of the hack. He must have realised that no-one used the facility and stopped checking.

"Steve, I need you to trace what the hacker has been up to. Check through the system logs and see what this Joseph has been doing."

"That won't be easy Paul." Said Steve "Joseph was defined three weeks ago, so that's when he got into the system. He must have been working for a while before that and probably regularly ever since."

"So?"

"We only keep the audit logs for two weeks. Anything earlier won't be on the system. The audits take up too much disc space to keep any more that the last two weeks. I can look through the system settings and see what he's left behind but I can't simply trace what he did from the audits. Most of them aren't there anymore."

"Shit! Well we know he didn't look at the e-mails until last night. That's when the return receipt was issued, so we can see what he has been doing for the past fortnight. With luck he defined the e-mail account and got side-tracked on another site until recently." He knew he was clutching at straws but he had to believe that a hacker wouldn't stay in their site long. He had to believe it, he simply couldn't see what anyone would get out of them.

"Check back for the past two weeks and see what you can find. In the mean-time we keep this to ourselves." Steve nodded his understanding. The last thing they needed was to have the directors in a panic. They had to keep things in proportion. Of course it was bad that they had been hacked but they couldn't have got any serious information. They certainly hadn't got any money out of the systems.

"Do you want me to shut him out of the system?" Asked Steve.

"Of course. No, wait! We need to see what he's been up to before we let him know. We have to find all the back-doors." He thought for a while. "We had better leave him for the time being. If he doesn't know we have discovered the hack we may be able to trap him." Paul was thinking fast, he had to develop a strategy to trap this hacker and he had to do it quickly and carefully, it was vital that the hacker, whoever he or she was, didn't know that they were aware of the hack at this stage.

"Get straight on those logs and let me know what you find."

Steve went back to his desk and started to look through the system logs. The first thing he saw was that they were only cutting the minimum amount of audit records, he simply hadn't increased the original system default settings, he hadn't got round to it. Still he should be able to see what this Joseph creature had been doing with the system files. Steve searched for the next three hours.

++++++++++++++++++

The previous February, in a Moscow gripped by temperatures 27 below freezing, Crazy Einstein had briefed his team, sitting round a table in their dingy back-street office drinking impossibly strong coffee. Outside, the dull roar of the traffic on Kutuzovsky Prospekt provided a curious contrast to the fairy-tale architecture of the city as the snow fell steadily on oblivious passers-by.

He had prepared a write-up of the project and they were all reading the brief. Crazy Einstein looked at them and asked if they had any specific questions. No one spoke, just a slight movement of the head as they concentrated on the job in hand. They were professionals, they took care of their reputation.

"The chances are that the security will be very good or very bad. It's unlikely to be in the middle." Crazy Einstein looked at the team for a while. "This is a small shop and while it's easy to secure a small site, many of them don't bother, so it will be a bastard or very simple. As always just be careful!"

The team members each had their own speciality and would break down the task of hacking the site into small discreet chunks. Once they were inside, and they never believed that they wouldn't get inside, they would make sure that had a number of entry points, just in case they were found out before they had finished the job.

The Christmas and new-year period had been really busy for OBSKURE, they had broken into a number of targets. They knew that it was an ideal time to get into any European company. Since then, and over the past weeks, things had been a little slow but there was always a steady stream of customers. This was the second job they had been given by Simon and it looked as if there were plenty more.

++++++++++++

Steve was working fast to see what the hacker had been up to. The first thing that puzzled him was why the IDS hadn't sounded an alarm when they had first been under attack. Even if the hackers had been able to get in, they should have triggered the IDS long before they had been able to get Paul's password. They would probably have extracted the password file and run a password cracker on it once they had the data on their own server. But Paul should have used a long and complex password that would take months or years to crack and he would have changed his password long before that had happened.

It didn't take him long to realise why the IDS would never have sounded an alarm, the hacker had changed the settings, at least he assumed that it was the hacker. The threshold of allowable events before the IDS would sound an alarm had been set so high that it quite simply would never sound an alarm. He knew he had set the limits far lower so the hacker had changed them. This meant that the hacker wasn't simply some 14-year-old 'script kiddie', although on the face of it that was all that was needed to seriously affect a large ISP that had recently been hacked. He knew what he was doing and this worried him. It suggested that they had been targeted rather than taken by surprise. The hacker must have wanted to get into their system.

He decided to see if there was a Trojan or Virus code inserted in the system. If 'Joseph' had targeted them it could be because they were a successful advertising agency. Some of the sicker elements in society aimed at companies like ASW. If this were the case, it may mean that the hacker, though good, was simply trying to disrupt the company, maybe the attacker was a loner after all. He ran the virus scanner against all the data and system files. There were several thousand to check, still he had to be sure. Just over an hour later, he was glad he had.

There were two system files that had been replaced with new versions that had been modified. The new versions contained additional code that would read and record any user account and password that was entered on the system. At a given command the file of accounts and passwords would be sent down the line to the hacker. This guy was good and it looked as though he had been in the system for some time. He checked the date that the system files had been installed and found that it was around the 25th March, it had been a busy time for the hacker.

Steve had a thought, maybe the hacker was someone they knew. It could be someone who knew the systems would be relatively unguarded. Someone who knew he hadn't got around to hardening the operating system. If this was the case, they would have time to work on their systems without any fear of being discovered. He then thought that if the hacker had been working most of last night, he could be looking for someone who was off work today. It seemed likely that the hacker had been busy for most of the night and there was a fair chance that they would not therefore be at work. He wondered for a few minutes, then another thought struck him. If the purpose of the amended system files was to record user accounts and passwords, there would have to be a data file with the information in. He quickly worked through the various operating system layers sorting the files into the order that they were last updated. There had to be a data file that had been updated today. After all, it would have recorded the logon of Paul and himself. He worked through layer after layer. At times like this he realised just how vast the Windows operating system was. There were thousands upon thousands of files. Fortunately, most of them were program files. He knew he was looking for a data file and while there was no guarantee that the hacker would have used any given file extension, such as .DOC or .TXT it was worth looking for these type of files first.

It took him about forty five minutes but he found it. A file called ASWNAME.TXT that was a list of every user account and password on the system. Steve looked in disbelief, at first he wondered why the hacker would have used such an obvious file name. Then he realised, it was only obvious once you knew you had been hacked. If he had seen it yesterday, he wouldn't have thought twice. "I guess you may as well use an obvious name. After all he would have found the file once he knew what he was looking for. An obscure name wouldn't have slowed him down much." He thought.

Steve thought for a while. His initial reaction was to delete the file but then he realised two things. Firstly, all that would achieve was not to give the hacker the passwords. He clearly had the ability to get into the system, so why would he need the passwords? Maybe for completeness? Then he had his second thought, maybe the hacker was working to his usual procedure. Maybe this was a professional hacker, someone who had been hired to get into their systems. Someone who always performed the same actions on every installation they broke into. He stared at the file of accounts and passwords. Why had the hacker called it ASWNAME.TXT? Why not just NAME.TXT? If the hacker were dealing with a number of companies, then he would need to identify which password file belonged to which company.

Steve had mixed feelings. On the one hand it meant that his security had been breached by a professional, so it probably wasn't someone he knew. On the other hand it meant that there must be something that a professional would be interested in. He had always been of the opinion that no decent hacker would break into their systems since there was nothing of real value that they could get. He wondered if the hacker really was getting further into their systems than he believed possible. No, the fact remained that the accounts and the client list was not on the system, so no matter how good a hacker thought they were they couldn't hack a computer that was not on a network. The accounts computer was completely stand-alone so Steve reasoned that the hacker may still be looking for the systems that he couldn't find because they weren't there to find. He smiled at the thought.

He looked again at the name file and decided that if the hacker wanted the user accounts and passwords, he would give them to him but decided that he would get everyone to change their passwords the next day so the old account details would be of no use! The hacker would almost certainly know the names of many of the accounts, so he would leave half of them unchanged but with false passwords. He would also add a couple of accounts and add them to the Intrusion Detection System. If the hacker used any of these the IDS would fire an immediate alert and he would know that the hacker was attempting to get back in. He made the changes and went to see Paul.

He explained what he had found and what he had done. Paul agreed that they stood a chance of catching the hacker if the IDS were now looking for him. He decided to 'crash' the system to get the hacker out. They re-booted the main server and, of course, the hacker lost his connection. As soon as the system was back, Steve changed the password of the Joseph account and removed the Admin authority. Steve had quite a backlog of 'real' work to do but for the rest of the day he kept an eye on the IDS system monitor to make sure that it was working. The hacker didn't attempt to re-connect. In a way he was disappointed but this simply reinforced the theory that the hacker was probably working on a number of systems. Maybe he would leave them alone for a while, or it could be that he had realised that there was nothing of real interest to get out of their systems.

Paul spent the day checking various e-mail accounts to see what the hacker could have got from the system but he was alarmed at the number of e-mails that June kept on the system. It seemed that she had rarely deleted any of them so the hacker would have been able to read all about their ideas for reducing the staff costs and they would even know who had been in the frame for redundancy. June really had let the side down, she should never have kept so much information on her e-mails.

About eight o'clock Steve called in to Paul's office to say that the systems seemed to be secure and he was going home to check a text-book that he had read at Uni about hackers and hacker prevention tools. He needed to get an early night and would continue the investigation again in the morning. Paul decided to stay on and work through the rest of the e-mail accounts. He needed to know what information the hacker could have got hold of. Steve left to drive his Mercedes home and Paul worked on in the quiet office.

It was around two hours later that things got really bad. He had been checking through the e-mail systems when he worked his way to Roland's e-mail he was old-school and usually wanted to send letters by snail-mail but to Paul's surprise he had embraced the e-mail system enthusiastically. The problem was that he had no idea about computer security or writing an IT Security Policy. Of course, that was why ASW had hired Paul and the rest of the IT people but even so, Paul had no idea just how bad Roland was.

On the invitation to the Christmas party, there should have been a map. Indeed, there had been a map but the map was for another party thirty miles away. Roland had intervened and said that he had posted a corrected map out to the Clients. In fact he had e-mailed them all so every single Client had been e-mailed by Roland. If anyone had been through his list of sent e-mails and had seen the large list of e-mails despatched with the amended map, they would have the details on every Client. That is itself was bad enough if he had followed the correct procedure. He should have used a group name for the clients so the individual names didn't show up on the "to" list. That was sloppy, but it got worse. They used TLS encryption between all of their clients and their server so the contents of any message was secure. The clients may be angry that they were known to other clients but at least they were all clients. What was really bad was the fact that Roland had sent a CC e-mail to his own Gmail account and that would have left the server without being encrypted. If he had sent this one to his home account, did that mean that he routinely sent company e-mails home? If that were the case, it meant that he was sending unencrypted messages to his private system.

Paul investigated further and was then appalled to find that on Roland's sent folder were a number of e-mails that contained audio and video clips, He had been sending advanced clips of forthcoming ad campaigns to clients by e-mail and then copying them to his personal account. The clips should have been protected but they weren't. Of course, many clips would be for current campaigns, so would only be confidential for a few days, some even less than that but Roland was responsible for some of their largest clients and these advertising campaigns would be "live" for months. Some of these accounts had spent millions of pounds on their marketing and these adverts were very sensitive.

The clincher was when he saw that Roland's userid was logged on to the system and working. Paul knew for a fact that he had left work early that day so that he could attend a formal function. This was serious, he had to get the e-mail server off-line. He had to shut it down. If this Joseph fellow had not yet read through all of Roland's e-mails and had not found the list of clients or the clips, there was a chance they could get through this thing. He had to take the initiative and take it fast. First he would cancel Roland's e-mail account, then he would start to get ahead of the game. He reached for the phone.

Steve was at home on the Internet when Paul called his mobile. He quickly explained to Steve just how serious the problem was and asked him how to close down the mail server. Steve looked at his watch and realised that the roads would be quiet so he decided to drive into work and turn off the systems himself. He said so to Paul and, to be truthful, Paul was relieved. He wouldn't have to take the responsibility of doing it himself. He could also get Steve to see if he could find any indication of unauthorised access to Roland's e-mails. He looked at his watch and calculated that at this time of night he could make good progress and it would be around twenty minutes before Steve got back to work.

Paul could feel the rising pressure in his temples, he knew the pulsating veins would be visibly throbbing his tension, like some biological Morse-code key sending out the details of his thoughts. He knew that he needed to be with Alyson more than ever as she would understand the pressure he was under. He could talk to her. If Steve came in quickly he should be able to sort out the problem and then rush over to Alyson. They could probably spend an hour together before he would have to leave and return to his wife.

+++++++++++++

Steve was making good progress, the traffic was light and the motoring gods seemed to be on his side for once. He'd had more than his fair share of green traffic lights, and even the usually militant cyclists seemed to be on his side. It was as if the urgency of the situation was visible for all to see. Steve continued past a row of recently refurbished shops. The reflection of the sleek Mercedes hopped and jumped in the windows of the trendy shops that he passed. He sped on and the car did the job that it was designed to do, it coped with the excessive speed on the corners, it coped with the heavy breaking. It was a miracle of modern design and ingenuity. It was a car for the less than brilliant. It could make the average driver look good, it could make the reckless safe and it could make the unwary seem prepared. It simply used it's many computerised systems to take over whenever the driver was about to do something dangerous, something that would put the car and driver in danger. As Steve was driving to work at a steadily increasing pace, the safety systems on the car were working overtime. They were averaging out his jerky braking, smoothing out his bad choice of line through a corner, they were doing what Mercedes had spent millions upon millions of dollars perfecting. Then, almost without warning, the magical systems in the car did the one thing they were designed not to do, they killed him.

Steve was driving at an alarming speed as the adrenaline was being pumped into his blood stream in ever increasing amounts. The ancient reaction to danger was designed to keep him alive; to give him the edge over an enemy, to allow him to react to a physical threat with increased strength. His brain was trying to stay alive. It was delegating as fast as it could, giving increased power to his limbs so that they could either run or defend him from whatever danger he was facing. The problem was that the responses that his brain had triggered were no longer needed. He didn't need more strength or extra stamina he needed to remain calm. He certainly didn't need to have his time perception changed. One of the effects of adrenaline is to seemingly slow down the passage of time. The problem with this is that if you are trying to get somewhere fast, you constantly seem to be slowing down. This is what was happening to Steve as he drove in to work. He felt he wasn't going as fast as he should. If he had looked at the speedometer, he would have been shocked but the effect of the adrenaline and the computerised systems on the car was to smooth out the ride and make the car seem to be travelling slower than it was.

He pressed his right foot down for the twentieth time and the car increased speed. He was working his way through a twisty section of road that passed some light industrial units. One of the units had just taken a delivery of office furniture and the lorry was pulling back on to the road as Steve approached. The driver of the lorry didn't hear the speeding Mercedes approach and Steve didn't see the lorry until it was far too late. As he rounded the corner, the lorry rapidly came into view. It was completely blocking the road and Steve instinctively slammed his foot on the brake. The computers of the Mercedes snapped into action seeming to say. "I'm taking over, you can't possibly want to break as fast as that. We both know you'll crash the car if I don't help."

So the computers took control of the situation and prevented the car from losing control. The problem was that this was one of those rare times when the car needed to skid out of control. The computers were keeping the Mercedes and Steve on a steady course but the course led through the side of the lorry. In a lesser car Steve would have been skidding across the tarmac and slamming into the building on the opposite side of the road. He would have been hurt, maybe fatally but at least he would have stood a chance of living.

In the Mercedes, the computers kept the braking system under control preventing the car from skidding and they were sending Steve at great speed into the steel girder running the length of the side of the lorry. The seat belts in the car were tightening, the wheels didn't lock and the car was on a steady course. He sat helplessly as the car hurtled into the truck as his brain pumped adrenaline into his blood-stream. He watched as the bonnet of the car hit the side of the lorry. He heard the cacophony that was the collision but he was powerless to do anything about it. His head hit the side of the lorry and in an instant, he forgot everything he had ever known.

The crash continued and the damage to the Mercedes increased as it slammed under the side of the lorry, but there was no-one to care anymore. For the second time in his life, Steve had put his faith in technology as a replacement for common sense and as a result he was dead and Paul was waiting impatiently for him to arrive at work. He wouldn't arrive of course but Paul couldn't know that. If he had he wouldn't have been thinking such ungenerous thoughts about Steve. Still, Paul would have the rest of his life to feel guilty about what he was thinking.

As for Steve, he had just **had** the rest of his life.

+++++++++++++

It would take almost an hour for Paul to hear about the death of Steve but by that time he guessed that something was seriously wrong. Once Steve was more than ten minutes late, Paul began to sense that something was wrong and when he was twenty minutes late he knew that the lack of any message meant that there was a problem. Even so, the news, when it came was a real blow and it took several hours for Paul to realise just how much he had depended on Steve. He wouldn't be able to depend on him now.

Chapter 4

"Good evening, is that Paul Taylor?" Asked a voice on his mobile that he didn't recognise.

"Yes, who's that?"

"I'm PC Wilson. Are you expecting to meet Steve Jones?"

"Yes, he should have been here some hours ago, what's happened?"

"I'm afraid he has been involved in an accident sir and I saw that you had called him shortly before he left his home, so I wondered if he was on his way to meet you."

"Yes, I'm his manager at work, we have a problem and he is on his way in to help fix it. Is he all right?"

"I'm sorry to say that he has been in a collision and has been killed sir. We have been able to contact his parents, we got their number from his phone, so we sent a car round to tell them. As your call was very recent I wondered if he was driving to meet you, so we wanted to let you know that he will not be coming in and to establish the details of his journey."

There were some more questions and an exchange of contact details before the call came to a conclusion. Paul wasn't much good at grief. He tried to get the right tone in his voice.
"Oh, thanks for letting me know." Was all that Paul could manage. He ended the phone call and sat feeling completely numb.

Paul couldn't believe that Steve was dead. Steve, his best technician thought Paul. Get real, Steve wasn't the best anything, he simply was just the most compliant, the one you could bully into working weekends. Shit, he was the one he could rely on in a crisis and he was dead. He felt numb, stupid.

Paul looked out of his window to the streets below. They were so different from the way they looked during the day. Business people frantic to get to a meeting were replaced with a less frenetic crowd as they were enjoying an evening out

Paul looked down at the folder on his desk. He really did need to get some help. He realised that he was in shock. The whole scene was dream-like and he almost expected to wake up and find that it was all some horrendous nightmare. He expected to wake up but he knew that this was real. This was what he was being paid for. This was why he had the big office and the fancy title. This was what paid the mortgage. He snapped back to the situation. The fact that the computer systems were being hacked as he sat there. The fact that the hacker had read the most sensitive e-mail that he had ever sent. The fact that an e-mail about possible redundancies in his department had been read by a total stranger. Or was it a stranger? Was it someone that he had met, someone who worked for a competitor? He felt the rising panic in his body and he had to get a grip on things. He had to stay in control.

He looked at the folder and saw the name Laura Billings, someone he hadn't seen for a few years but who he knew would have the experience to help him out. He dialled the number on the top of the letter-heading. At first he thought that she was out, since there was the sound of her voice-mail message but then he remembered that she always let the calls go through to voice-mail so that she could ignore any calls she didn't want to take. He started to leave a message when the phone was picked up.

"Laura, Hi - its Paul Taylor, from ASW, the Ad Agency"

A moment's hesitation and then Laura answered. "How are you?" A question that she meant. She was the complete opposite of the usual City type. Laura was plain speaking, too plain for some people but as she and the handful of associates she worked with were very well respected she was never short of work. They were all specialists in their field. She was a security and network specialist that Paul had used when he worked at a previous employer and they had a problem at their German office. Laura had been brought in to identify the problem and resolve it, something that she had done very quickly. The upshot was that the Germans were impressed and Paul had come out with his reputation as a problem solver firmly established. This time he would be content just to keep his job.

They chatted politely for a while Paul asked her if she was still into classic cars and bikes. "Yes, about six months ago I bought a 1968 650cc Triumph Bonneville. I stripped it down to the chassis and have restored it. It is great fun, even though it's a bit slow compared to a modern Japanese machine." He smiled, he had almost forgotten her engineering degree and the fact that her first love had been for all things mechanical before she has discovered the joy of working on computer networks. At 5 feet 7 she was only just tall enough to ride the classic British bike but she was also very slim and that meant that her weight was against her if she needed to manoeuvre the bike in a tight space, like a garage. But as they chatted he remembered the first time he had seen her, he thought she was there to introduce the next speaker. When he realised that she was the speaker, he waited to see if she knew what she was talking about and after about 5 minutes he realised that she was very good.

Laura asked Paul how he was keeping. "Fine thanks, it's been a while." Said Paul. "Last time I saw you was when I went on the Internet Security course I think. You were giving a talk on Network design and segregation."

"Yeah, wasn't that the seminar where you disappeared on the last day?"

"Er, could have been, I had an important appointment."

"Oh well, I hope she was worth it, anyway, what can I do for you?"

Paul outlined the problem. Actually he outlined the main problem, i.e. the hack. Laura thought for a while and suggested she get straight over to ASW to see for herself. Paul said that he would prefer to see her in the morning. For the time being he had shut down the e-mail system and the Internet server so no-one would be able to get in, they would simply assume that the system was down. Paul hurriedly made some notes so that he was sure to have the facts straight ready for when Laura arrived. He also checked through the system logs to extract evidence from the main accounts. He printed the original registration of the Joseph account and the return receipt for the e-mail that had tipped him off to the original problem.

He knew he couldn't speak to Sebastian, since he was at that fancy dinner and would certainly have his mobile phone turned off. He could do no more until the morning.

++++++++++++

38

Paul was in the office just before 8 o'clock the next morning. As soon as Sebastian arrived he went in to see him. Seb had a simple policy, if his door was open anyone could walk in to see him but if the door was closed it meant he was busy. The door to his thickly carpeted office was open and he was sitting behind his large antique Partner Desk.

"Sebastian, we have a serious problem." Paul tried his solemn voice as Seb looked up from the Financial Times that was opened flat on his desk. "I'm afraid that Steve had an accident last night. He was killed in a car crash." He was looking at Seb, for whom the colour had completely drained from his face.

Seb was an older man and also had a son just a few years older than Steve. He sat and looked at Paul with a blank stare on his face. "Oh my good god" he said slowly.

Paul continued "I heard last night. He was coming back to the office to work with me on a project. His car was travelling fast and he hit the side of a lorry as it reversed out of a factory gate. I think he must have been killed instantly.

"What terrible news" he said softly, "Has anyone contacted his parents or next of Kin?" and after a pause added "And does June Know – she was particularly fond of him"

"I haven't yet, but the police had already checked his phone and he had an "ICE" number." Seb looked puzzled. "It means "In Case of Emergency" and is an entry that the police look for to give contact details, so I assume his parents will have been told. I am just about to go through to June and get her to invoke the company procedures, or whatever they do in this situation" Paul was getting uncomfortable now. He had never had a personal conversation with Seb and he was clearly moved.

"The problem I have now is that I have lost all of the documentation for the new system. Steve had it all in his head and he didn't have time to write it all down."

"That sounds bad." Said Sebastian solemnly as he stared at a point on his desk that seemed to be just below the surface.

"It is bad but not critical. I phoned a consultant I know and she has agreed to come in today to help out."

"Is she good, this friend of yours?" He asked absently from deep within himself.

"Yes, she's not a friend, just someone I have worked with over the years." Paul said rather too defensively.

Seb looked at him "OK Paul – I am sorry to hear this, do whatever you think is necessary and let me know what is done for Steve and his family, you know, with the funeral arrangements etc, and make sure I am kept fully informed. Oh and tell June to ensure that the company insurance and pension details are not protracted for whoever is a beneficiary"

Paul nodded and left the room as quickly as he could to leave Sebastian to his thoughts.

++++++++++++

Just over an hour and a half later Laura called to say that she was about five minutes from the office. Paul gave her directions to the private car park that ASW used, and then he waited. Six and a half minutes later, she was standing in Paul's office. He would have recognised Laura, though not at once. She had changed her hair style and colour but as soon as she spoke, the old Laura was standing in the room.

The last time he saw her she was in office-casual attire and eager to impress. Now she was successful and didn't need to the image was one of a cross between The Girl with a Dragon Tattoo and a Camden Market stall holder. Black jeans, boots, wild hair, big bulky donkey jacket, black roll neck sweater and little make-up. The odd piercing and small tattoos on her hands and face set it all off. She looked a lot younger than her 34 years, but he knew that inside that mind was a sharp, intelligent and experienced brain that stood no nonsense.

She smiled at his reaction. The look had the desired effect. She had a dry sense of humour and was known to be straight and deliver her no nonsense opinions with no bias.

Paul liked the look and the person wearing it. He began by outlining the situation.

"I need to check the settings on the firewalls, and the perimeter defences and make sure that the operating system has been hardened. Do you have a listing, or should I check the settings on-line?" Said Laura after she had listened to Pauls briefing..

"I set up an admin account for you while you were driving over, here are the sign-on details." Said Paul, handing her a post-it note.

"By the way, the hacker, is he still on the system?"

"No, I shut everything down last night and so far he hasn't attempted to log-on yet. Of course, he could log-on at any time." Paul looked at Laura.

"True, but let's deal with the most pressing problems first." Paul had waited for her to log-on to his PC. She looked at the display for a few seconds and then entered a number of commands. The account of Joseph disappeared off the system. She had deleted the account and made sure that all files and data bases relating to the account were saved as evidence or for possible future use.

For the next ten minutes Laura constantly entered command after command. Paul sat and watched from a distance, not wanting to break her concentration. Finally, she turned to Paul and asked.

"Where do you store the offline audit files? I can see the online ones but they only contain about a week's worth of records."

"We don't bother to keep them. As the web-site is just a shop window, we don't have any sensitive data to attack, so we didn't see the point in using machine cycles to process and store records that have so little value."

"OK, you seem to have an Intrusion detection system that's connected to the Firewall, I can't see a HIDS or NIDS."

Paul's blank expression said it all.

"OK, HIDS is a Host based Intrusion Detection System and NIDS is Network based Intrusion Detection. These are designed to block unauthorised access at the host and network level. They give far more flexibility than a single, and I must say, rather old fashioned IDS. But I assume that you don't have either?"

"No, we were relying on the Firewall to block a hacker."

"Most decent hackers would try not to be noticed by a Firewall unless they wanted to shut the systems down, in which case they will try to overwhelm the Firewall. Your IDS is OK but if a skilled hacker gained access and then used a compromised account to change the system settings, you simply wouldn't have a clue."

"Where's the documentation for the system?" She waited for an answer and for a while she mistook Paul's expression so she continued.

"I need to see what the system settings should be so that I can check what they are now, that'll tell me what they've changed."

"I'm not questioning the need for you to see the documentation Laura, it's just that we have only just upgraded the system and haven't got round to documenting the settings yet."

Laura shot him a look that would have breached most arms limitation treaties.

"OK, we don't have any documentation. Steve has it... I mean, Steve HAD it all in his head."

"So you've no system documentation and you've had a major incident. Most of my mortgage has been paid by companies that didn't document their systems! Do you have an inventory of hardware and software?"

"Not as such. I can speak to Accounts and get a list of the hardware we have paid for."

"So if I look at your servers and see an application, how will you know if it's a valid piece of software?"

"Well, we would recognise our main applications."

"I'm sure you will but would you know ALL of the software, the apps, the utilities, the one-off pieces of software that any user has bought? Or any software that a hacker has installed?"

"Yes, with Steve dead…" His voice trailed off for a while. "We will have to re-create it." Paul finally admitted, as much to himself as to Laura.

Laura had been switching between displays on the PC and had just about seen everything that she needed to.

"Paul, are you OK to give a hand? I know that the death of Steve has been a real blow but you are in quite a hole and we need to get on top of what's happened and what's happening right now."

"Sure."

"Good, if you do can list all of the e-mail accounts. I'm assuming that you will know all of the accounts that you should have, is that right?"

"Yeah, there should be around twenty-five to thirty, no more than forty." Paul said. At least that was good news. If there had been two to three hundred, or more, it would have taken quite a while to check that only the valid accounts remained on the system.

"Good, I'm going to look at the Firewall definitions and the IDS. I need to check that they haven't put in some entries to allow them to come and go without raising an alarm. I will then define the valid accounts to the IDS so that any other one will not be allowed, and I need to check that they haven't opened an obscure port in the Firewall to let them come in that way, in short I will be looking for a back-door."

Paul was impressed. It may take a while to put all the definitions in place but it would mean that the IDS would be on their side, even without a HIDS or NIDS for the time being. It would warn them if any other account were used, even if the bogus account had been hidden deep in the system. With the IDS sounding the alarm, it would be hard for a hacker to remain hidden if they were still on the system.

By mid-day, Laura had a pretty good idea what the hackers had been doing. She was now sure that there had to be more than one hacker. ASW had been the target of a professional attack, of that she was certain. The hack seemed to have been well planned and that meant it wasn't a random opportunist attack. It was deliberate. It was, almost certainly, paid for by a well funded individual or organisation and if that was the case, they must have had a clear objective in mind. The fact that this was a professional attack put it into a different league from an amateur crime. The other factor that worried Laura was the time-scale. If the hack had begun three weeks earlier, maybe four, then they must have had some sort of a result. Most hackers would have pulled out if they had drawn a blank, or at least only spent a few days looking.

While Laura was working through the IDS, Firewall and operating system settings, Paul was listing all of the e-mail accounts on the system. It didn't take him too long since he knew the accounts off by heart. When he checked, he found that there were four false ones. They had all been defined around the same time and three of them hadn't been used yet. They were obviously there as backups in case the original "Joseph" account was discovered.

One of the accounts was a previously valid account belonging to a retired Director. If Paul hadn't been looking, he was sure he would have missed that one. The fact that it was based on a previously valid account suggested that the hackers would expect it to remain. They would probably only use the account to create new accounts if the original ones that they had defined were discovered and deleted. It was clear that whoever was behind the attack was taking some serious precautions. They had done their homework and Laura suspected that it was a team that had worked together for a while.

Now that they knew the extent of the userid problem, the next step was to see if there were any back-doors planted in the system. To be absolutely accurate, they needed to see WHAT back-doors had been put in there. It wasn't possible for someone as careful as their hacker to have overlooked the necessity of keeping a way in. Any competent hacker would make sure that they could get back into the system any time they needed to.

Laura explained to Paul that the e-mail receipt he had seen was sloppy, as if the hacker was being complacent. She also pointed out that there was quite a lot of work to do to harden the system and make sure they had tracked all of the possible back-door code. She suggested that the next day, she would bring in two of her colleagues to help with the task. At first Paul wasn't too keen but in the end he realised that this was not the time to try to cut corners. They had to protect the system and do it fast. If not, the hackers could get back in and plant a whole new set of back-doors. They would be back to square one! Laura left Paul to monitor the IDS for any new attempts at gaining access.

The next day Laura and two associates arrived, Paul defined new accounts for them and they started to get to work. They ran a scan of the system to list the missing patches and put them into priority order. The report was checked and a long list of missing patches identified. The operating system was examined to see what settings had been missed off and the Firewall rules were listed. These would take some time to check through but it was a job that had to be done.

Laura then worked her way through the report and started to test and install security patches for both the operating system and application software. She was looking for any of the well known and not so well known exploits that she expected the hackers to have made use of. She was also looking for any code that they had inserted into the system... The hackers had planted about twenty bits of code in the system. Some of the code could be triggered remotely; others would be triggered by a specific event, such as a date. The idea was that the system would keep making contact with a command and control centre that the hackers were using to communicate with their system. This gave them their first breakthrough. It meant that they may be able to identify where the hackers were based. With any luck, they would be a team based in the USA or Europe. If she was extremely lucky it may be a hacker group that she had heard about from her time trawling the Dark Net. If she got lucky she may be able to work out the motive behind the attack.

It seemed that things may be starting to go their way. Laura looked at Paul and explained the strategy. Paul was impressed. Sure they had been hacked but if he could recover the situation and tell the rest of the Board that the hackers had been stopped, or maybe even under arrest, he would turn out to be the hero of the hour. His euphoria lasted nearly fifteen minutes. That was as long as it took Laura to realise that the hack was far more distant. She guessed, though at this stage she couldn't know for sure that the hack was coming from the old Eastern Bloc. It was possible it was coming from Russia itself. If this were the case, there would be no chance of getting anyone arrested. She had been looking at the time stamps on the data files. During the week, the hacker seemed to log-on early evening, once he was sure that everyone had gone home. This made sense. Yet at weekends, the hacker liked to log on earlier, as if he wanted to give himself as much time on the system as possible. It was the recent Bank Holiday that gave Laura the clue. "You would have thought that the hacker would have made the most of it."

Yet when she had checked the time stamps, she found that the hacker had not logged on to the system on the Holiday Monday until the evening. It was as if the hacker hadn't realised that it was a bank-holiday in the UK. Furthermore, when she looked at the IP addresses that the hackers had connected from, many were hidden but a few had connected from Russian servers. It looked as though the hackers had been surprised that they hadn't been seen and become a little over confident. Instead of hiding their true IP addresses, there was one of the hackers who was probably using an internet cafe, or a public Wi-Fi hot-spot to connect in.

Laura gave the news to Paul. In fact the news was mixed. On the one hand they would not be able to have the hackers arrested. On the other hand, the attackers wouldn't be in a position to complain if ASW took the offensive and started to attack the hackers. While this was most unlikely to yield any results, it was possible that the hackers could be caught off guard. At least it was worth a try.

So far they had deleted the accounts and for the time being the hackers hadn't attempted to re-connect. It was possible that they were simply busy on other 'customer sites'. It was worth a try. Laura was going to re-define the accounts to the system and then add them to the Firewall. If the hackers attempted to log-on, the Firewall would drop the line. At the very least it would annoy the hackers. It would let them know they had been seen, it may even put them on the defensive. If nothing else, it would feel good to have the hackers on their back foot for a while.

Chapter 5

Laura had worked for about 12 hours a day for nearly a week analysing the situation and trying to set up traps and routines that would help identify and track the attackers. There was little else she could do and even then she did not know if they would try to get back in.

Their reaction depended on a lot of things. If it was a planned and co-ordinated attack, the type that Laura always feared when looking at Computer Security Breaches, then they would have taken all they wanted early in the attack and would be trawling for only tit-bits at this stage. Any sign that they had been discovered could mean that would have withdrawn and closed down all their activities.

At 7:30pm Paul had sent out for a take away meal, coffee and soft drinks for them all and they had eaten well, if not the most healthy of meals. Laura's associates were working their way through the mass of missing security patches. Laura and Paul were now sitting in his office talking over the hack and its potential to damage ASW.

"One problem is of your own making" said Laura "You have designed a web-site that you use as a brochure for ASW. You don't sell over the Internet and you don't store customer data, so you thought you didn't need to conduct penetration testing"

"How do you know that?"

"Paul, me and my colleagues have been looking at your system and the mass of missing patches. Any decent pen test would have seen what we have seen and as you seemed to be surprised at my initial findings I assume that I was giving you news, hence the lack of pen testing."

"OK Laura, but the fact is, we don't have any customer or payment data on the site, so I don't see what the hackers were after."

"Well there could be three issues. Firstly, you do have valuable data within your network, even if it isn't available through the web-servers but secondly, your web-site can be taken over and used as a command and control centre for criminals to use in DDoS attacks. It could be used to send Spam risking your reputation through your IP addresses being seen as Spam senders or, God forbid, your servers could be used for serious criminal activity. What if you found that you were hosting the next terrorist plans or illegal music or films for downloading or even worse, illegal porn? You simply can't leave your servers open for any hacker to use as he or she wishes. The third issue is that your web-site can be a way into your network, even if you're not trading."

He knew there was a certain amount of "head in the sand" attitude about it but he never saw ASW as being a hacker's target. Yes companies had their web-sites defaced and there was the occasional story of a large fraud being committed via a web-site or online transaction, most of which, Paul noted, were facilitated by an insider or someone with insider knowledge. But he never saw ASW as a fraud target. They just did not have that type of profile or systems.

Paul had always seen the biggest threat as coming from inside. It could be a disgruntled employee who deleted something or ordered an item using a company purchase order that had already been authorised and then amended the records. In fact most damage to IT systems came from ignorance or accidental use, and as far as he and his team were concerned that was all about backups and the ability to restore them quickly. A slight annoying thought then struck him that it was a long time since he tested the contingency procedures and he must ensure that someone was still looking after this – they might need them after this episode.

There was the occasional long silence in the room.

Paul was thinking about the effect this would have on ASW and more importantly his career and standing within the company. He had worked hard to get where he was and saw this comfortable position at ASW as a reward for long days and nights in the operations and project management roles he had held at other companies.

He had been given a lot of responsibility and had built a fine team that was good to work with, even if it was small with Anne, Steve and Janice, the intern. The memory of the death of Steve arose again and he still could not believe it. The job had enabled him to travel, choose his own priorities and make important decisions. He had also met Alyson at ASW and she was just about the most exciting thing that had happened to him.

Paul had been married for 15 years to Sonia, a girl he had met in his first job after leaving University. She was a computer programmer in his first company and it was a case of common interests, common backgrounds, common careers and lust. They were married 18 months later and Sonia had given up work soon after to have their first child.

That child was now a 14-year-old son called Jake who Paul referred to as "Kevin" in memory of the old Harry Enfield character. 4 years after Jake was born, Sonia gave birth to a girl, Katie and this girl was the apple of Paul's eye. At 10 she was bright, sporting and mad keen on the latest pop idol, the name of whom he simply couldn't remember, they seemed to change so often at her age.

Alyson was the Financial Director's secretary at ASW. She was 26 years old, slim, sexy and very ambitious. She had made a beeline for Paul at their first Christmas party just after they had completed a particularly large IT project and he had wanted to unwind too much. They had both had too much to drink and ended up making love in Paul's office just after midnight. They had been doing the same thing twice a week since, not in Paul's office these days but in Hotels, Alyson's flat and over the occasional weekend when Sonia thought Paul was at a seminar or User Group meeting somewhere.

Laura was spending the time trying to analyse the actions and estimate the type and nature of the people that had attacked ASW. She knew only too well the different types of hacker there were out there. She had been one of the key participants on a CERT (Computer Emergency Response Team) task force that profiled these attackers, assessed their motives and objectives and then developed a program to watch their progress on the internet to assess their danger to British computer networks.

Laura sighed and broke the long silence. "What you have to understand Paul is that the information available on the Internet is expanding at an ever increasing rate. You can find information about a company and what they do for a living and that is good. You can find information about an individual and that may be good or bad, depending on your intention and you can find information about how to conduct a criminal or terrorist act. Anything from building a bomb to how to hack a computer along with the exploit script that you would need to take advantage of the vulnerability is available. And remember there has never been as much information available as there is today and there will never be as little information in the future as there is today. The strange thing about the Internet is that it makes everyone equal. We all have to obey the same set of rules and we all start on the same level field of play."

"A good analogy here is the road systems. It doesn't matter if you drive a large articulated lorry or a small electric town car. Nor does it matter how much your car costs or the speed it is capable of. We all have to drive on the same road systems and we are all subject to the same speed restrictions and traffic dynamics. Sure the laws may be different in each country but if we don't obey some common standards like, which side of the road you drive on and how to turn right or left then the whole system grinds to a halt."

"It's the same with the internet. There are a large amount of people out there with nothing better to do but play on the Internet and have fun. They share information, become knowledgeable on how systems work, how to fine tune them, repair them and even break them"

"In fact – to continue the analogy, there is every type out there from the opportunist thief who steals a car that has been left open or with the keys in the ignition, through to the joy-riders and then up to organised teams of people that steal cars for profit and resell then elsewhere in the world."

Laura smiled at her own analogy as she had recently had her classic Porsche stolen from outside an office in Oxford. Now she was driving a five-year-old Ford that no-one looked at twice and certainly didn't want to steal. To her surprise it had every bell & whistle she could want and a responsive engine to boot that transported her around in very fast luxury. All that for about eight grand. It was strange but she realised that the reason the Ford didn't sell had nothing to do with its equipment – simply that it didn't project the right image.

She continued, "It's the same on the Internet. There are the sad gits in attics somewhere who just play the virtual teams or clans who hack just to get their names on the bulletin boards – similar to the graffiti artists- right up to the closed-rank and very dark attack teams that do this for a living. They hire out to anybody who wants to pay them to hack anything – Networks, PABXs, ATM's. Some even do it for political ideals."

"How will we know the motivation here Laura?" Asked Paul. "I'm beginning to worry now that it is not just mischief".

"OK" said Laura. "Let me take you through what I know or can guess and see what we have"

Laura thought for a while. "They would have been researching this for some time Paul" he said. "Teams like this will carry out considerable research on the internet to glean any info they can about the potential target and remember that they have found your list of e-mail accounts. From that they can use a script to search for each of the e-mail addresses. "

"I don't know how that would help them – we are very low profile. Just the web-site and the odd press mention, not much about our systems" – Paul quickly responded.

"Well if you search for "@asw.mail.com" as an advanced search or use an aggregated search engine, like zoo.com that uses other search engines, you can sometimes get some interesting results. So if the hackers were looking at a site like www.linkedin.com to see which of your employees has a profile there, they will probably have found some of your IT people. Do you ever use contractors, other than me of course?" He smiled.

"From time to time we do, the last one we brought in to do a specific job was Steve Smith. We used him about 3 months ago."

"What did you use him to do?" Asked Laura.

"He was a consultant techie we had in last year for a month contract to configure our firewall and IDS and to train Steve Jones, my technical manager" Replied Paul with a stab of sadness and guilt. It would take a while to get over his loss.

Laura entered his name in quotes in Google and had a few results that looked interesting.

"Well I hope you didn't pay him too much, he is asking simple set-up questions on your Checkpoint Firewall. Look at the quality of the responses, they quite plainly think he is incompetent, this one here is telling him to RTFM." Laura continued, she looked at Paul for a response and when one did not happen she explained; "Read The Manual" – and grinned.

"Seriously though" Laura continued, "think about it – it tells the potential hacker that – One, you are using Checkpoint products – so forget the exploits and open doors in the other type of firewall. Two, that ASW don't know much about it and, Three that Steve Smith is a contractor – he even mentions it in the body of his question, and look here! He ends up by telling the world what type of Intrusion Detection System and Servers are connected to the firewall".

Laura sat back resigned. "Its like an open invitation to have a go at the site" – she said.

"Shit" muttered Paul, "I see what you mean". He thought for a while. Quite apart from hiring an obviously incompetent consultant – again a CV had blinded him – I must make sure we don't leak any further information. Even the list of e-mail names - firstname.lastname@asw-mail.com is a hint or clue to an internal userid. His train of thought was interrupted by Laura.

"I hesitate to ask Paul – but do you have any kind of written standards or policy that relate to security, data integrity or – dare I say it – secrecy?" Laura looked at Paul's face and immediately knew the answer. "I thought so! – Well that's something for the future. It's the simple things Paul" she continued, "length, structure and age of passwords, using your company e-mail address on bulletin boards for ANY type of communication, Ownership of userid's – by that I mean ensuring that people are responsible for their logon details and don't easily give them away. Honestly – if people looked after their corporate details and data in the same way they looked after their ATM pin codes and bank accounts numbers I would be out of work."

"I know, I know" Paul interrupted, "It's not easy being told to lock the barn door when you know that it is an easy thing to do and you always gave other tasks a higher priority". He looked at Laura and his shoulders dropped. "All this is known Laura – it's just that we didn't know how easy it was to hack and, more importantly, how easy it was to hack us!" He wandered over to the window and for the tenth time that day looked at the London skyline and wished he was in bed lying next to Alyson and able to forget this nightmare.

Paul and Laura had previously talked about the number of vulnerabilities that existed on the Web Server platform that they used. In the ASW hack it was a simple buffer overflow attack. This involved typing in a very long string of characters into an input field in the web application and overflowing an Input buffer. The effect was to cause the application to abort and leave the browser user looking at a blank page in the directory that the application was running. The attacker would then be able to execute commands to list the contents and execute any programs that were in that directory. All input should be checked for content and length and only valid characters should be allowed through. If you have a name field, then you shouldn't allow a $ or / to get through and it should be limited to, say 22 characters.

Further access to the c:\ directory was obtained because of the lack of security, restrictions or permissioning to use other areas of the hardware disk. The attacker traversed to the root directory of the server and could look at the whole disk and its contents. In this case there was a security system in place but the Password file was kept in a system directory, which was unprotected.

The normal procedure is to encrypt the live password database with a common system utility supplied by the manufacturer. This meant that conventional password crackers could not easily crack it, provided that the password was strong. However, if you chose a short password or one that only contained lower-case letters, then it could be cracked in a reasonable time-scale.

Paul had enquired how they would have obtained a copy of a password cracker and Laura explained that it was a simple matter of loading one down from a web-site that gave them away, or you could buy one that would be used for genuine "password recovery" when a critical system had been protected and the user had forgotten the password that they had used. Of course, there is no such thing as software that "knows" when you are recovering a password for legitimate reasons and will prevent the criminal use.

Laura went on to explain that for example - L0phtCrack - is a password auditing and recovery tool designed for Windows operating systems. It is billed as a utility to allow system administrators to audit the strength of the passwords their users are using. With it a password file in Windows can be tested and the time taken depends on the structure and length of passwords and the algorithms used in encrypting the passwords and the cracking algorithms used to break them.

The full crack of a password file, when run against L0phtCrack, can take a very long time, and depending on the length and structure, can sometimes never be done. First a known list of passwords and a dictionary of words is used against the file, and then it uses a brute force attack using every permutation of character string to break it.

If a standard word is used, Month, day, country, Noun, then it will be cracked in seconds by using the internal dictionary. If the length is 6 characters and only lower case alphabet characters are used the brute force attack will take just under 2 hours.

The maths is simple. Given that there are 26 characters in the alphabet, then multiply by 2 to cover case sensitivity. Add 10 for the numeric values, and maybe 8 to cover the special characters that can be used, so you have 70 possible options per password character. If a 10 character, gibberish password is created using all the available character types and the cracker is run on a mid-range machine that checked 50,000 passwords a second, then the crack could take between 300 and 25,000 years to check every possible permutation. BUT hackers don't use the Central Processing Unit (CPU) to run these attacks. They use the Graphical Processing Unit (GPU) that is used to run the powerful games. A GPU will process many times faster than a CPU and you can chain GPUs together. A single GPU will run as around 12,000,000 tries per second and when they are connected the result is that a password cracker will often run at over 30,000,000 tries a second, so a password of 10 characters will give you 70 to the power of 10 possible passwords, that's 2,824,752,490,000,000,000 which is 2.8 quintillion possible passwords. And that's a massive number. Now divide that by 30 million tries per server per second and you get 94,158,416,333 (94 billion) seconds which is 2,984 years. However, on average the cracker will find the password in half that time, so you have 1,482 years and if you have hacked into a number of large companies where they each have 3 – 4,000 servers you may be able to put 10,000 servers on the job and crack a password in 108 days. But remember that they will try a simple dictionary attack on every user. The chances are that they will get several passwords in the first hour.

He turned to look at Laura. "The way they got in to the system Laura – is it common?"

"The use of the exploit and what vulnerability was used is not the problem here Paul" said Laura idly twisting a pen in her hand - it was the kind of subconscious action that a person develops when they have spent a lifetime waiting for one computer function or other to finish. If Laura had a 10p piece for every minute she had watched a Blue Bar fill up waiting for a processing task to complete - she would be a wealthy woman, though given her skills and the number of companies that didn't know how to protect their networks, she was already fairly comfortable!

"The fact is" she continued, "that given the state of the hardware and software that is let loose on the business community at large, there will always be front doors, back doors, trap doors and gaping great holes for criminals to use to get into private networks"

"Also don't forget the massive server farms that Communications Providers such a BT, Vodafone and TalkTalk use to run their internal systems and external operations. Typically these companies run many thousands of servers which have to be maintained and serviced. Then they will reach end of life and have to be replaced. In one of the many seminars and user groups I attend I overheard a Security manager admit that they have actually installed servers, and by that I mean more that 10, with the default Admin userid and password left unchanged. Can you imagine that! The attacker has to simply know or browse the default User/Password combination and try them – and he is in!

Paul was appalled but managed to smile. "I'm beginning to believe that." he said. "You said as much last time we met and even then you said it would get worse". Laura had de-briefed the team at the last company that Paul worked at and made constant references to the number of vulnerabilities being found in hardware and software.

"Yes it has - Paul, and it will continue to do so until companies, or more specifically the IT teams in the companies start to take security seriously. For example just go to the www.cert.org or www.cert.gov.uk for the UK website – that's a Computer Emergency Response Team that acts as a centre of information and Internet security expertise which is operated by Carnegie Mellon University in America or the UK Government here. Look at the number of vulnerabilities that any of the research sites are reporting. And if what I have read about the number of holes in the latest operating systems with Windows, Linux, Apple, Android etc - things are likely to get worse. Operating systems try to be user friendly but in the process, they include so many 'friendly' facilities that getting the bugs out of the programs is impossible. Most commercial operating systems contain millions of lines of code, how on earth are their development teams meant to fully test them?"

"But with the growth in platforms it is surely going to get worse" - Paul said looking surprised. "What on earth do they need that many platforms for?" He knew from previous experience that earlier versions of windows did not have anywhere near that much code. For example Windows 95 had 10 million and then Windows 98 had 13 million. The resultant user benefits had always been a little obscure to him.

"Let's not forget BYOD, which I think stands for Bring Your Own Disaster. Every personal device should have a standard set of applications, the same operating system and be fully patched. There are products out there that try to segregate the work and private areas of the user device but there are ways around the 'sandbox' as it's known." She said.

Laura thought for a moment. "I know it's a catastrophe waiting to happen, and do you know what Paul? All that they have done is give us a rewritten and less reliable system which has more holes and more bugs than ever before" She smiled ruefully, "and for what? Just the ability to use and build the same spreadsheets, PowerPoint presentations and word processing documents that we have been using since 1994. Oh - and don't forget the wonderful whizzy web pages we can view! You know the ones that take ages to appear and in doing so use active X or Java-Script that runs in the browser session for the PC to use. Think about that for a moment. We are allowing code to be executed on a server somewhere that executes on our PC's to deliver more functionality! – That's on top of the operating system, browsers and applications software, all of which have security vulnerabilities that need to be patched on a regular basis," she shot Paul a quick glance." The security risk alone is mind boggling."

"So" - Paul deliberately drew a line under that train of thought – it was all too depressing. It meant that they were going down a track where the same mistakes and situations were bound to occur. "Once they were in and had the passwords for the web server – what then?"

"Well this is where it becomes a mixture of using the systems that are bad and your own office practices." She said looking at a distant point on the wall and was careful not to adopt a 'Told You So' attitude.

"From the web server you can see every other server in the network. File servers, print servers, application servers and the mail server. The firewalls in place simply did not restrict access or create any kind of safe-zones. In fact once they were in they could pretty much see the entire network. The only systems they could not see was your financial and accounts system. Whoever took the decision to isolate that completely from the rest of the network has done you a big favour"

"That was Sebastian the MD," responded Paul. "He was under great pressure from Bill Rayfield the Customer Liaison Manager to keep things separate. Bill is Old-School IT. Grew up with mainframes and is always stating – *Well in my time it was easier to secure, backup, use, - whatever.* He drove us mad!"

Bill was one of those old style IT guys who was hired by Seb a many years ago. He didn't report into Paul but directly to Seb and acted as his Consigliore for all matters relating to Customer relations. Paul did not know but he suspected that Seb hired him as a favour to his wife who knew Bill's ex-wife. Whatever the reason, Bill was very popular and had integrated well into the company.

Laura smiled, "Yes I know the type. And do you know what? I completely agree with him. It seems that we have done nothing to improve the usability, reliability and integrity of these systems we have delivered over the years.

She continued. "Anyway, once they were in it was simply a matter of connecting to the server and trying the userids and passwords they had cracked. The tragedy of this is they all applied to all of your servers. It is very common for systems people to use the same userid and passwords for all access. They even sold products a couple of years ago to promote it – SSO (Single Sign On). It's at this point Paul that they would have been treading very carefully. They had cracked the crown jewels and they then needed the time to trawl thoroughly through your systems and look for the information they were after. The last thing they wanted to do was trigger alerts, leave footprints or degrade the performance of your systems to the point where you noticed."

Laura sighed. "The first thing they would have gone for is the e-mail server. You use a package that allows anyone with full admin access to read any e-mail folder. So every personal, business and corporate e-mail would have been scrutinized.

"So they simply crawled through all of our mails at leisure and took copies of what they wanted!" Paul said almost to himself, trying to come to terms yet again that his precious system had been completely compromised and all the corporate data had been compromised. Every time he thought about it he got a pain in his head.

"Bloody hell" he blurted, "what an almighty mess" His outburst was not entirely due to the corporate data being stolen. He cringed when he thought of some of the personal e-mails he had sent to Alyson, commenting on the many nights they had spent together and what they did. She was a sassy little thing and liked it when he talked or wrote dirty... "Shit!" he thought – I hope that stays private.

"After that" said Laura – ignoring Paul's reaction "they had a number of places to go – File servers, application servers, any desktop that had been left powered up. I notice that it is a common practice to simply let your screen saver click in and leave the computer logged on until the next morning."

"Yeah" said Paul, "that or just Log Off and leave it at the Log-In screen. I even do that myself sometimes. It takes so long to power the machine up and wait for the log on screen that it's easier to leave it on. Also we have pretty good physical security here that it didn't seem a problem"

Laura nodded in agreement, "The fact is Paul that most people feel that way. It is slightly different in a big open plan office where there are a large number of people around who could use your PC for any purpose, but in a small office it is not seen as a risk. The real problem is of course the fact that if it is left on and hackers are inside then they can get onto your PC hard disk and trawl around without anybody knowing. There is another problem Paul, I see that users are encouraged to keep video clips on their own computers and not on the main servers. This means that even if you had a good level of encryption on your static data, the files on the user's own computers would probably still be stored in clear. You need to take responsibility for all your data and get the users to store everything on the servers. That way you can protect it and back it up."

She went on without stopping. Laura was in full swing now reading from notes. "To my mind the main area they would have gone for is the application and business servers. It is there that you keep all of the creative and media applications and where you prepare and develop the output for your clients. I had a look around there earlier and there are a number of presentations, video clips and research charts and customer outlines relating to the various customers. Thankfully the customers are all given code names and that data is well hidden with a need for some client software to be able to use and analyse it."

"OK so what do we have?" Paul said after a long silence.

"The bottom Line is" Laura let the sentence hang and looked at his notes.

"You have the web server compromised but not defaced" she looked up at Paul, "you may want to get your web people to go through it with a fine tooth comb or simply reload the backup version – assuming you have one! I see that Anne is your main application developer, does she also look after the web-site?"

"Yes, she is very experienced."

"So did she design the web applications?"

"No, Steve designed and wrote them before Anne joined us."

"Well I suggest that Anne is asked to look at the design and make sure you improve the input validation. That was where the hackers were able to get into the system. While they did tunnel in from outside, if that had failed, they could still have got in through your web-site. Get her to check everything. I have seen very simple word changes take place on a web-site that can compromise a company's legal position, rubbish a rival or impact your brand image"

She continued "The mail server has been completely accessed – so assume all mails have been read and any data sent in or out has been captured. That's the beauty of mail packages they allow you to use them as some sort of personal filing cabinet so that if you lose a file that someone sent you and you saved the e-mail it is still there ready to be extracted" Again she looked up from his notes, "ask your people to declare any usage of mail that will cause you problems – not an easy thing to do but honesty is needed at this stage".

Laura stopped and looked at Paul for a brief moment as if to form the words he was about to say. "Paul. I need to brief you on a delicate matter"

Paul looked at Laura alarmed. His mind was racing. Was he going to mention his e-mails to Alyson? Laura had not met or did not know Sonia. He looked at Laura expectantly.

"Your Finance Director, Malcolm, how old is he?"

Paul was taken back for a few seconds. "Mid fifties I guess, why?"

"When I was looking at his e-mail account, I discovered some old attachments in his sent folder that were quite large. They contained several video clips and a number of still images that would be defined as pornographic. In fact they were mainly Gay images that he probably downloaded from one of the many web-sites"

Paul smiled. "Oh my god, did you look at them?"

"I only looked because some of the attachments were quite large and even then only briefly and I must say that they were fairly harmless, in that they were clearly adults engaging in 'physical and fantasy banter', if you get my drift. So there's no suggestion of the images being illegal. But my first thought was how did they get on the system. Do you have any browsing or e-mail filtering software to prevent this type of image from getting onto the system?"

"No, but I have made it clear to all staff that they must only send valid company information on an e-mail. He has clearly been ignoring my instructions. I don't care if it is 'legal' porn, no-one is allowed to send ANY private information in an e-mail."

"So what written policies do you have that will deal with is situation?"

"Well, nothing written down but everyone knows what the rules are." Paul said.

"I don't think you understand the situation. If you haven't written a policy and made sure that people have read it, then there is NOT a policy. If an employee saw anything that they may consider offensive, and you have allowed it to be sent, then the company could have a harassment claim against it. But it could be even worse. It is only recently that it has been legal to be gay, for most of his life, people of Malcolm's age would be breaking the law if they engaged in a gay relationship and that would lay them open to blackmail. It isn't enough to simply pass a law, Malcolm may still see a social stigma associated with being gay or even having such feelings. It will take some time before society sorts out its attitudes. After all, how long has it been illegal to discriminate against anyone based on their race, gender or religion? We have a long way to go and Malcolm may be vulnerable to undue pressure and given his position he must be supported, but you need to ensure that all employees know what the rules are. Also remember that I only looked at a handful of e-mails, I didn't look right through his messages because of the confidential nature of his job" She paused to let Paul think about what she had said.

"Right where was I? – Oh yes - every File server and desktop has been investigated, except the Director's machines or personal areas, with the exceptions of a few of Malcolm's e-mails. You will have to make arrangements to look at those yourself at some time Paul – it's normally outside of my brief. We have to assume that these criminals have been in the system during the day also so any PC that has been used is likely to have been compromised, the only data that would be safe is where it is not resident on a server and the PC has not been used for the duration of the illegal access."

"Finally all application data must be deemed to have been copied or browsed, except where a particular piece of software is needed on the PC to view it. And even then we cannot assume that the hacker didn't have that client software on his PC"

Laura sat back in his chair and frowned. "Not a very good story is it? It is a good thing that your financial systems were isolated so that is a plus" Again she looked at his notes

"And now some final comments ...

One – there are no current backups of data so if it was a malicious hack and they corrupted or deleted everything you would be up Shit Street...

Two – There is no way that you could bring a prosecution against these people – even if we discovered who they were and if they resided in this country. This is because there are no relevant audit logs or access statistics to use in evidence against them. You cannot detail who used what, where and when. Furthermore you cannot establish what they did with it and if it was amended"

Laura looked up from his notes. "Paul, if only people would log and audit their systems and maybe use one of those new central audit products that would enable you to cross reference and analyse access across networks this type of hack could be detected and analysed"

"Finally, you need to remember that the hackers gained entry through the network. The security controls were poor but we have looked at the applications, though only briefly. It seems that your web-site may be vulnerable to direct attack. A skilled hacker could probably inject system commands directly into the comments field on your web-site. You don't seem to have any filtering on the data that can be entered. I suggest you get your developers to read-up on securing the web-site by design. Get them to look at preventing SQL injection (pronounced sequel). Also have them check up on preventing cross-site scripting. If you simply harden and protect the network, you will still be very vulnerable."

She put her notes down, "And please remember that I've only looked at the network, I haven't looked at the applications in any depth, so I can't judge the web-site or your back-end systems but other than my findings, I think you're in fairly good shape! One question though, do you make use of the free help that is out there for small companies?"

"No, I wasn't aware that there was any."

"Actually there's quite a bit. Have you heard of the Cyber Security Clusters?"

"No, I can't say I have."

"Well ask Google for your local one. They are groups of companies and consultancies that are there to help small companies. There are a number of them, then there's the British Computer Society or BCS, they aren't just for the large IT departments and there is the CISP, that's run by the government and the police and then there are some good publications dealing with Disaster Recovery and even Disaster Avoidance for small business. Finally there is a publication from the government called the 10 steps to cyber security."

"Well thanks I had no idea there was so much advice out there. A few years ago there was nothing." Paul said with a rueful smile. "I presume that you will be detailing this in a report for me" Paul was thinking about how he would brief Seb on all of this.

Paul sat back in deep thought, and then said "What a shambles... How did we ever get in this situation? All we wanted was to use these systems to get on with our job and we seem to have developed a monster that we can't handle. How could they let this happen? How could they give us systems that let in the hackers?"

"They!" said Laura bluntly "is you, Steve, and everyone who wants to use simple systems and easy ways of managing and controlling the IT hardware and software that you buy." The pen stopped spinning in her fingers and she look Paul straight in the eye. "You want fast powerful cars that get you about quickly and safely, but it's those same cars that get used to joy ride, get away from robberies and kill innocent people!.. It's the same argument as the arms manufacturers. It's not guns that kill people its people that kill people. It's people that hack other peoples' systems and they will use what they can find, beg, borrow steal or even develop to do just that! In your job you should know that they will come after you and design your systems to keep them out where you can, and alert you if they do get in"

Paul knew the argument and accepted in his own mind that Laura was right. It was up to him and people like him to realise this and factor it into his business plans, budgets and infrastructure. He had just buried his head in the sand and prayed that it would never happen to him. Of course he took the normal and reasonable precautions but like everyone else that drives and leaves their cars in public car parks - he just reasoned that accidents, events and chance would never affect him.

"So what I have to do then" he looked out of the window at the city roofline. "Is to put forward a case for hiring or contracting in the expertise to harden our systems using the up-to-date patches and upgrades from the hardware and software vendors, and regularly assess our vulnerability to attack using an outside agency." Paul continued to look at the sky and city roofs and began planning the words and phrases he would use to persuade Seb that he had to spend more money on this problem. I have to tell him the bad news on the hack, especially after the shock he has had over Steve's death, and then tell him he has to spend money on ensuring it does not happen again. He will go ballistic.

Laura looked at him guessing the thoughts that were going through his head. "Well" she broke the silence. "In the short term that is your only course of action, but there is another way to go about this"

"And what is that – resign? Paul retorted quickly.

"Maybe" Replied Laura just as quickly. And Paul shot her a look. "No, seriously, let's look at the situation you find yourself in, you've been chasing your tail and that has given you a number of problems. You can choose to simply use the technology that the company needs rather than chasing the latest fad simply to be at the leading edge. You could start to use IT just to drive the business."

Chapter 6

Laura settled back in the chair and started to spin the pen in her fingers again.

She was now on her favourite subject. Talking about the use of IT in business and the many, many examples of good and bad practices that she saw in the course of her consultancy.

"They started here in ASW – back in the 1980's putting together the systems that your business needed to compete and trade in "today's" technology driven world or rather what it was back in 1985. At that time is was probably a small mid range computer that handled nothing more than your advertising campaigns, invoicing and maybe some bought and purchase ledger. In those days the systems you used were just automation tools that enabled quick and easy manipulation of accounting data. The systems were provided by probably one or two of the manufacturers of the day plus some tailored software that specialist people could use."

"When you think about those times – computer security never existed. The main security was the lock on the computer room door and the recognition of the carefully selected people that operated and used the equipment."

"The driver for installing this IT set-up was productivity and cost savings. You could do more work, write more business, and process and track more invoices with less people" She took a breath.

"The type of systems – programs, techniques, procedures - that were developed then to enable data to be input, stored, sorted, queried, changed and printed – at first on paper, but nowadays on browser screens, are still valid. In fact many of the back end systems that large banks and insurance companies developed then are still in use"

She stopped and looked over at Paul. "I will give you an example here. The insurance companies addressed the motor market traditionally via brokers and in the high street or by post via the old style insurance agents who went from house to house– The Men From The Pru, and of course in those days they were all men. One company broke the mould and introduced a Direct Selling application to the public via the telephone. All you had to do was call a number and immediately you could be covered on your car. This company – Direct Line Insurance, knew that they had to choose a stable, fast, reliable and secure IT system to handle the kind of market sector they were after. So they looked at the systems available and rejected most. They rejected the new, multi-platform, untried open systems that were available and chose instead an older mainframe technology supplied by companies like IBM and Hitachi."

Laura stood up and walked slowly round the room. She had a habit of doing this at her seminars to emphasise various points.

"This technology used a large "mainframe" computer with closed connections - that means only accessed by strictly controlled hardware terminals that performed in a set and structured manor - dumb terminals – and connected them directly to the central processor. The objective was to have operators sit at these terminals, answer the phones and use fast, reliable and secure systems to write the business directly with the customer. I used them once and they answered the phone within three rings! – no automated call centre and multiple choices. Then I spoke to a well trained lady who took me through a series of questions and insured my car in 8 minutes."

Laura looked out the window and waved his arm, "As you know they have become a major success and changed the way people buy car and house insurance.

Paul looked at Laura. He had heard the Direct Line story but he had not realised the significance of it. "Are you saying we should move to that same technology Laura?"

"No" Laura replied quickly "what I am saying is that they choose the best business solution that was available. They chose the right tool for the job."

"OK maybe Direct Line doesn't fit in with the technical flavours of the day, proposed by the pompous, overpaid analysts and their fancy magic quadrants. Nor did it impress the modern techies and the PC / Server knowledge they brought with them from University, but it did the job! And it still does. If it ain't broke don't mend it!!!"

"Paul - how many times have you upgraded and replaced your systems in ASW to simply do the same job – support the business?" Laura stared at him and Paul's face answered the question.

"Oh don't start me on that one Laura. We have been on the Upgrade Escalator ever since we converted our systems from the midrange boxes to this Client Server environment sometime back in the early nineties – before my time here. It was the same story at Banke Nederlande, when I first met you. Always chasing our tails upgrading or improving the systems and chasing a bottleneck round the network"

"We have just about become stable on one system and started to think about stability, change control or the introduction of acceptance testing of a new system and someone has a knee jerk reaction to something and off we go again, upgrading servers, desktops, operating systems, office suites. – We had to upgrade from Office 97 to Office 2000 because we couldn't read the Word or PowerPoint attachments that were being sent to us by our customers. When I spoke to James Pemble over at PK Components – at the time one of our biggest customers - he said the same thing, he thought it must be a ruse started by Microsoft."

"Do you know that we once upgraded to the latest server release just to keep a techie from moving to another job? He wanted experience on that software and we wanted to keep him. OK we were planning to move to that release at some later date but we pulled it forward to keep him. His CV drove our requirements. I wonder how many companies know that they are in this position without realising it."

Paul continued – he was in full swing now. "We put an application package in last year for the creative media department. It was developed by a specialist company and cost us a fortune. It had no security, no update or maintenance procedure and the bugs we found! I am sure they tested it on us and let us Quality Assure it. In the end it took some four months to introduce and that included a PC upgrade for all of the relevant users. That system cost us £1.7 million in total to implement and for what? Just so we could run video clips on our PC's and automate the project management of the new advertising campaigns".

Paul smiled to himself. "Then the Creative Director left to go to our main rival and one of the reasons they wanted him was because he had experience on this particular package – crazy"

"The end result is that we may be leading edge but we are always fire-fighting problems and bugs in these systems rather than maybe improve the system documentation or in this case ensuring that the systems are secure and hardened"

Laura smiled. "Yes Paul – I have always thought I was in the wrong job. Some of those guys that sell hardware drive the latest BMW's or Porsche's"

Paul smiled and said, "Yes Laura but you did drive a decent Porsche!"

"True, but I'm good at my job and I deliver value for money, not like some of the overpaid sales people."

Paul glanced out of the window and his own BMW. He remembered talking to one or two of those salesmen at MBA Software, the company that sold them the creative media suite. One of them had a particularly nice BMW with all the latest extras and proudly took Paul and Seb to lunch in an expensive restaurant. It was partly that ride that encouraged Paul to push Seb for an upgrade to his car last year.

Seb had just returned from a trip to the Monaco Grand Prix, courtesy of the same company and Paul had been unable to go due to implementation dates of the project. It took a bit of manoeuvring but Seb finally Okayed an upgrade to the 5 series beauty he drove now. In a strange way Paul felt a sense of pride when Steve picked up his new Merc following that good review. How quickly that all disappeared when the news of Steve's death came in.

Paul thought back over the past few years and some of the decisions he had made. They say that hindsight is the only "exact" science and certainly when he looked back; some of the decisions were wrong and driven by anything other than what the business wanted. Paul had a particular twinge of guilt at the times he had made a decision to attend a product launch or seminar just to spend time with Alyson on the evening before.

Laura continued. "You know I was once a guest speaker at a sales kick-off meeting for a hardware company and one of the marketing guys gave a presentation on selling to existing customers."

Laura was always being invited to present at seminars, users groups and sales meetings to inject a level of humour and cynicism into the proceedings. People loved the stories she told about famous hacks and stupid business decisions that resulted in some type of catastrophe or other.

It wasn't hard to do. If you looked at the level of middle management in most large organisations it was surprising any of them survived. She had lost count of how many decisions had been made on the basis of saving their backsides, pressure or persuasion from vendors and how good the experience of implementing a product, service or system would look on their CV.

"Yes" she continued, "they asked me along as a guest speaker and because of the agenda I sat through a following presentation that was being given to the sales force."

Laura became animated and pointed at Paul to emphasise the point. "I was absolutely astounded at how little respect there was for their customer base. The main theme was that existing customers are the easiest method of generating income for the least amount of effort. The title of the slot was "Upgrade for Growth" and it centred on how to manipulate their users to upgrade to the latest, and of course chargeable, versions of their software."

Paul was nodding and knew exactly what she was talking about. The amount of times he had argued with pushy salesmen on the cost of upgrades and increases in maintenance charges.

"In fact I always use my tablet with a voice recorder app on it. I say that I want to record the conversation and placed the tablet in the middle of the table. If a sales person objects I ask why and if they agree I find that the meetings are short and have much less sales waffle in them."

Laura poured herself some coffee from the thermos jug and sat cupping it in her hands, deep in thought.

"IT has spent the last 30 years moving from one fad to another. Hardware, apps and operating systems shoot into fashion and then fade. Most of IT is aimed at the large to mammoth companies and governments that seem to have almost unlimited budgets to chase the latest fashion. Of course the people who work in IT are always looking to make sure that they have the latest and most desirable skills. There are under 10,000 large companies in the UK, companies that have a large IT department but there are over 5 million small to medium companies with an average IT department of less than 10 people and they simply don't have the number of staff to employ the specialists that are needed to keep an IT department up to date and secure. Yet IT as an industry doesn't seem to understand this. The medium size company must be really smart in order to use their budget wisely and also avoid both the upgrade trap and falling behind. It is a fine balance that they need to tread."

Paul smiled. He remembered the interviews he had been sent to by the head-hunters who wanted a share of the silly salaries that were being offered by major multi-national companies in the City. Paul had attended a few of them and was shown into flash west-end offices that were being financed by venture capital and listened to the inexperienced eager young directors telling him what a success this was going to be. Heavens knows what decision they made with regard to hardware and software but it was a penny to a pound that it was the latest version of everything that they were installing to build these wonderful systems.

As if to read his mind Laura broke the short silence again "I was invited by one or two of the trendier companies to consult on their network security. One particular company that was intending to launch an online share dealing site had asked a security company to perform a penetration test and application check on their Web Site. It was torn apart!"

Laura smiled and looked at Paul with an incredulous expression on her face. "They had built a web application that allowed you to buy shares online and once you had a quote for a price there was a 15 second limit to that price. You had to buy in that time period or the quote became invalid. The only trouble was they had loaded the code that controlled the 15-second window down as Executable Code on the PC. All a competent person had to do was capture the code, change the 15 seconds to something much longer and get another quote on a stock that was rising. Then they could wait until it had gone up and buy at the original offered price. Bingo – an instant profit. Of course I doubt that the Stock Exchange would allow the sale through its checking procedures but the point here is that the code was nearly live at this site and I know that several other web-sites were using the same type of code."

"It was obvious to me Paul that many of the web-sites and applications that were in use did not address the security or data protection issue at all. I never put my credit card number out over the net unless the site is UK based and I check that the company is based in the UK. Anyone can use 'co.uk' on their web-site, no matter where they are based. Even then I use a separate card with a low credit limit on it."

Paul nodded – It was true. The level of programmers that were out there looking for jobs was very surprising. Some had good degrees and could write decent code but their understanding of the needs of a corporate system was often poor. They expected the end user to tell them exactly what to write, including resilience and security. Paul had interviewed some of the would-be analysts and developers for jobs at ASW and quite how they justified the salaries they had been on, he did not understand.

"When you think about it" Laura was walking and talking now "Even the large banks and Insurance companies fell into a similar trap. They had been using older, well established mainframe and mid-range systems – what we called Legacy systems" She stopped and grinned.

"Do you know Paul in the USA the word 'Legacy' means something good that your relations or parents have left for you in later life! In the UK it means the opposite. As I was saying, they took these systems and then integrated them with newer Client Server or Web Based systems and created a complete business application with them. The problem was they were designed to do different things. The older systems were designed to be used in a different business scenario that maybe included call centres or other manual procedures. When they were integrated with immediate access systems so that the customer could enter the web-site, register, choose, buy and have immediate access to the service like House

Insurance they became subject to subversion, fraud and very embarrassing events that could damage their image."

"I worked with many companies to uncover scams where badly put together applications that integrated browser code and front-end servers with 'legacy' applications and databases had gaping great holes in them. OK so maybe they did not suffer any loss but the amount of times the attacker could break out of the application and damage the site was unbelievable"

They fell into another silence – each deep in thought.

"OK Laura, I am convinced" Paul stood up and paced the room. "We have been manipulated and pressured by the vendors, forced by our own staff, blinded by our own ambitions and needs, and persuaded by industry trends. Here we are with systems that are becoming increasingly difficult to manage, not cost effective and leave us with problems of security and integrity and we find ourselves in this situation! We have been hacked over a period of time and there is a possibility that most or our corporate data is compromised."

"How do I brief Seb about the bad news, ask him for a budget to make our systems secure and then tell him that much of what we have done in the past is wrong!"

Laura stood up and looked straight into Paul's eyes. "If I know anything about managing business Paul it's that you have to give Seb the Problem and the Solution"

He walked over and looked out of the window as Laura spoke. "Being hacked is a big problem as we don't know who has done it and for what reason. We know it was probably planned rather than being an opportunist criminal, we can be fairly sure of that, as far as we can ascertain, there was no damage or vandalism of your systems and we have a fair idea of exactly what they have seen and possibly copied. Also we know what they haven't seen."

"If they choose to do nothing more, then all we have to do is close down the holes quickly, learn the lessons and get on with our jobs. And guess what? Part of doing that job is to ensure that we manage our systems better and build a manageable cost effective IT environment that is secure, reliable and the correct tool for the business"

"Paul, what you have to do is lay out both the short term plan of hardening your systems, and the long term plan, and this is where you cover the cost and get a return on the investment, which is to properly manage your IT and deliver only the systems that the business needs. This might mean a radical rethink in how those systems are put together and how they are run, but the end result would be an IT set-up that delivers business functionality and not technical functionality."

Laura Looked at her watch. 01.23am. "Oh hell Paul, I am getting too old for this!" she smiled. "I think we have done as much as we can here tonight."

She looked at Paul with genuine concern in her eyes. Poor Sod – she thought. He is not a bad guy, just trying to do his job and the rug has been completely pulled from beneath him.

"I will compile a factual report for you Paul and get it to you ASAP. As usual it will be aimed at board level and it will be hard hitting. In it I will outline a lot of our findings that we have covered in our conversation here tonight"

Laura could easily promise this, as it was a series of words and paragraphs that she had used many times before. In fact almost every site that found themselves in this situation had suffered their fate for exactly the same reasons. They had simply failed to install and manage the correct IT infrastructure and thought that "It would never happen to them". It took a shock like this to make them sit back and look at what they had done to get here.

"I will send you a draft of it before it hits you officially so you can prepare a response, or should I say defence" She looked at Paul with an apologetic smile.

"OK Laura – I wouldn't have expected anything different" Paul knew that Laura operated with the utmost ethics and respectability.

"I will have to prepare very carefully how I tell Seb about this whole thing and have my case fully rehearsed."

Paul stood up and packed up his things. He walked Laura down the stairs and out past the lifeless security guard on the front door.

They both walked to their cars and drove off in separate directions into the night.

Chapter 7

Malcolm was short, too short. When he got angry he leaned back in his high leather chair and allowed his legs to swing. Most men could push themselves back in their office chair with their legs and keep their feet on the ground. Let's face it, most children could do that but not Malcolm, he liked to have his chair raised up and he was simply too short. When he leaned back in his chair and let the executive leather super deluxe most expensive chair in the company lean back, his feet would leave the equally expensive carpet. The moment you saw Malcolm you knew he would have the most expensive chair in the company, he was that type. He was also the Financial Director, the man in charge of the purse strings.

Right now he was leaning as far back as the chair would go and he was swinging his legs. Now the way that Malcolm swung his legs could tell you a lot about the man. If he swung them in an alternate pattern, one in front and one behind, then he was lost in thought. This was rare. You knew that despite his head for figures, of which he was, it has to be said, extremely good, he had no imagination. The fact was that any thought that wandered into Malcolm's head was doomed to die a terrible and lonely death. If, on the other hand his legs were swinging in unison, both together, then he was agitated and that, even by Malcolm standards, was not a pretty sight.

His little legs were swinging now, swinging in unison and swinging with such force that his big executive leather chair was recoiling three inches at the end of each swing. The out swing saw him move three inches nearer the desk and the in swing saw him move three inches away from the desk. The recoil was silent of course, the deep carpet saw to that but he was swinging his legs for all he was worth. The reason for the swinging legs was a phone-call that he had taken about four minutes ago. The call was from one of ASW's rivals WILLIS & SPACH, and they wanted to know if the Board would consider a take-over of the company.

WILLIS & SPACH were the only other agency in the country that could come close to ASW in terms of creative thinking, public relations and customer relationships. It was known that they had tried to poach several senior staff in the past, in particular Roland Carter. Malcolm also suspected that Paul Taylor had also been approached, as the

WILLIS & SPACH IT network was known to be crumbling and they had problems hiring.

It was following an earlier approach to Roland that Seb had restructured the company and allocated the shares to the key members of the ASW board. To date Seb had kept 20% of the shares he owned and allocated 15% to Malcolm, 15% to Roland in the hope of keeping him, and June and Paul had 12.5% each and kept 25% spare. In all Seb owned around 30% of the ASW shares, so even with passing on so many, he was still a powerful man.

Malcolm and his legs were indignant and believe me when I tell you that, Malcolm could be very indignant indeed. He was a control freak. That's why he loved accounting systems, he absolutely loved being the Finance Director of ASW. Most accountants enjoyed being able to maximise the company income. They know that they can produce good profits, reasonable profits or a healthy loss from the same figures, within reason. It is the love of the figures that drives most accountants, that and the fact that it is a well paid job. Malcolm was different, he loved the control. If he weren't an accountant, he would probably have been a salesman where he would believe his natural personality would shine through. He would, of course, spend his life being thrown out of job after job but he would never be able to admit that he had been in the wrong. He would be the salesman from hell, with his shiny suit and his over-sized car, which he would drive far too fast for his abilities. So, all things considered, the general public should be grateful that Malcolm had gone into the accountancy profession. Even ASW had benefited from his talent, it's just the people he came into contact with on a daily basis that felt uneasy. The people on the end of the phone seemed not to be enjoying his choice of profession right now though. They had no choice but to talk to him, he was the Finance Director and they were talking money. The problem was that Malcolm was not in control of the conversation and this made him even more pedantic and sarcastic than usual. The representative from WILLIS & SPACH on the end of the phone was pushing Malcolm and his receding hair-line was glowing pink under the pressure.

Every so often, his legs would seem to try to do a double beat as his level of agitation increased. It was at the point that he realised that the voice on the end of the phone seemed to know as much about the worth of ASW as he did and that caused his agitation level to increase further. At last the conversation ended and Malcolm leaned forward in his chair to slam the receiver back in the cradle. He sat thinking for a while. He tried to work out how they could have worked out the true value of the company. How could they have obtained the figures? He simply didn't understand. Also and equally worrying was the fact that it was obvious that WILLIS & SPACH already had enough of the floated ASW shares to consider a takeover viable.

You will appreciate that this was not the best time for Paul to enter Malcolm's office on a mission of some delicacy. However, this is exactly what Paul did. To be fair, Paul was a little distracted himself, as he would normally have checked what mood Malcolm was in before deciding whether or not to mention a delicate matter. However, that particular day, things really couldn't wait. Paul strode across the room and sat in one of Malcolm's visitor chairs.

"We have a problem, Malcolm." Said Paul as gently as he could manage.

"And what is the nature of YOUR problem?" He asked, determined to make it clear that he didn't share Paul's collective responsibility.

For some reason, Malcolm was one of the few people that Paul had ever met who could annoy him within a couple of sentences. It annoyed Paul that he could do this and yet here they were, two Directors of ASW and they were about to start shouting at each other. Paul took a breath.

"Let me re-phrase the statement. YOU have a problem Malcolm." And before he could stammer a reply Paul continued. "During a glitch last night we had to re-send a number of old e-mails. Two of these were caught in the Firewall because of their size." Paul waited but Malcolm was listening and waiting for the punch-line.

Paul knew that Malcolm was not IT literate and was relying on the fact that he wouldn't know just how big a lie he was telling. He continued.

"As I was saying, two of the e-mails had attachments that were large. They were video clips and they were extremely obscene."

Malcolm then became unusually quiet. Paul had expected him to blow his top when he told him, in effect that he had intercepted two of his e-mails. Instead, Malcolm was sitting there as quiet as you like.

"What, exactly, was on these e-mails?" He asked.

"They were short pieces of film, extracts you may say, from a pornographic movie."

"I see and why are you telling me?"

"Because they were your e-mails, going to a friend with a Hotmail account." Paul produced two pieces of paper. "Here is a copy of the body of the e-mail."

Malcolm looked at the paper for a while and seemed to change mood.

"These e-mails are over two months old. How come you have only just seen them? In fact, how come you've seen them at all?"

"We had a problem with the mail server and a number of old e-mails got re-sent. The system then held them because of the date-stamps."

"Bullshit" Shouted Malcolm. "You've been looking at my e-mail file. What sort of 'problem' could possibly cause an old e-mail to be re-sent?" He was beginning to get angry now. "I want to know how you came to be looking at my e-mails!!"

"Calm down Malcolm." Paul paused and took a deep breath. "The fact is that last night we became aware that we had been hacked. I am certain that you're system has been accessed and we were looking to see what company data could have been copied. These two were very large, so I checked to see what the attachments were."

"I see and who exactly did the copying? After all, I know they are 'adult' images but they aren't illegal or anything. What is the problem?"

"Well it's mainly one of image. As the Finance Director of ASW I don't think it looks good for you to be sending out that sort of image, legal or not." Paul said as calmly as possible.

Malcolm started to lean back in his chair but obviously thought better of it. "The fact is I received the images from a mate…"

As Malcolm was speaking Paul was thinking that he was using a curious turn of phrase. He was sure that Malcolm didn't have any 'mates' as that made him sound too much like a 'bloke' a 'regular chap'. Malcolm was the type who would have 'acquaintances' but never 'mates'. His attention was snapped back to Malcolm's voice as he continued'

"…and the fact is that it's not the type of thing I'm into, so I sent it back. It's the return message that you've seen. I deleted the original of course."

"Of course…these particular e-mails aren't the real issue. It's the image of the company that counts. We work for a number of companies for whom image is everything. They won't care if you were returning the images or not, as far as they are concerned a senior director of ASW has been distributing pornographic images and they will probably take their custom elsewhere. However, given the nature of your job I didn't want to trawl through your e-mails, so I need to be sure that there isn't any sensitive data that the hackers could have copied."

"That's absolutely typical of you. The fact that the systems have been hacked is the real issue. My private and personal e-mails should be just that, private. The truth is that because you failed to do your job we may have a problem. I suggest you find out just how bad things are." Malcolm's pink head shouted.

"That's why I'm here. Tell me. Do you turn off your computer when you go home?"

"Yes, I did turn off my computer last night as a matter of fact." He shouted with more than a little relief.

"Well, not just last night actually. We are probably looking at the last three weeks." Paul said in quiet admission of the security failure.

"Three weeks, what the hell do you mean three weeks! Do you mean to say that you've allowed hackers to get into our installation for the past three weeks. You mean that they have been able to read my e-mails for THREE WEEKS!" He was obviously angry but there was more to it than that.

Paul was equally angry now. "Yes, that's exactly what I'm saying. Now answer the question. Do you turn off your computer as you have been told to?"

"Not every night, no I don't. It takes so long to turn on in the morning that most nights I leave it turned on. I switch off the screen though."

Paul gave a snort of indignation. As if turning off the screen would make the slightest difference. "Well then, it's not just your e-mails with their attachments that they have seen. It's anything that you've sent by e-mail and kept in your 'sent folder' or on your computer."

Malcolm was suddenly very quiet. He looked at Paul and then down to the framed photo of his mother on the corner of his desk. "I suppose that's how they got the figures."

"Who got what figures?" Asked Paul.

"I had a call from WILLIS & SPACH and they seemed to know our financial situation down to the last penny. It must have been them."

"Well that's one thing they can't have got. The accounting system is on a completely separate part of the network. All the work you do on that can't be seen from the main systems because we have a separate area."

"But the computers are in the same room." Stammered Malcolm.

"No, the accounts are on a system that is protected from the rest of the network and requires a separate sign-on, the real issue is what do you hold on your computer? I think I had better have a look and see what they have got hold of." Said Paul attempting to get control of the situation.

"NO!" Shouted Malcolm. "Don't avoid the issue. I don't understand how WILLIS & SPACH got our figures. If they got our e-mails then they must have been able to get the figures."

"Don't worry about the accounts, they really are protected, they only exist on the accounts server and that is linked to the separate computer in your office and to your assistant's computer. I'm more concerned about what you have in your e-mails and the contents of your main office computer." Paul was getting agitated and the atmosphere was about to deteriorate into a slanging match.

For once it was Malcolm who tried to calm things down. "Bear with me Paul, you're the computer expert but I would have thought that anyone who could get at the e-mails would be able to read the accounts. If they can, then that explains how WILLIS & SPACH got hold of the figures."

"OK Malcolm, I'll explain, the accounting system exists only on the accounts server. When you sign on to the main systems, including your e-mails, you can't access the accounts without doing a separate log-on. You are connecting to a separate part of the network. The programs aren't on your office computer are they? It therefore stands to reason that the figures must have come from some other source. You are sure that the accounts only exist on the accounting department server aren't you?"

"Sure, I have the figures here and at home, of course." Malcolm stated flatly.

"What do you mean by 'at home of course'?" Asked Paul in a quiet voice.

"Well, I have a copy of the accounts at home on my computer there. That can't be a problem, the only connection to that computer is on a secure broadband router and that is password protected" Malcolm smiled the smile of someone who had just demonstrated that he knew far more about computers than Paul realised.

Paul looked at Malcolm as the colour drained out of his face. "Tell me Malcolm, how do you use the figures at home? The accounting system only exists on the office computer, right?"

"Of course it does. Steve had previously explained all about the licensing issues. He said that I couldn't have a copy of the programs at home." He paused and decided to explain from the beginning. "Look, about a year ago mother was ill and I needed to spend a few weeks at home." He looked at Paul for a sign that he knew what he was talking about, Paul nodded. "Well, I needed to keep in touch, so I asked Steve what he could do for me. He explained that I couldn't connect to the accounting server from home and I couldn't have a copy of the programs at home but he could download...Is that the right word?"

"Yeah, download is fine, but download into what?"

"Microsoft EXCEL. He said that if he converted the data to a spreadsheet format I could use it on my home computer." Malcolm smiled a smile that was definitely not returned by Paul.

"Let me understand what you're saying. You talked Steve into providing the accounting system data in a format that can be read by some 80% of the world's computers. Data that started life in a format that could be read by 0.00001% of computer systems. Do you, by any chance notice a slight reduction in security there?"

"Well, Steve didn't say anything about security. How am I supposed to know?" Asked a very indignant Malcolm.

"So, how does the accounting data get to you? I suppose you write it out to a USB thumb drive?" Paul was trying to match Malcolm's arrogant tone but failing, he was getting far too angry.

"No, we looked at using an encrypted USB but my tablet doesn't have a USB slot. Steve suggested that I use a CD writer and encrypt the data."

"Well at least that would be secure. So that's what you do, is it?"

"No. I don't have a CD reader on my tablet either."

"So what do you do then?" Asked Paul with growing apprehension.

"Simple, I attach it to an e-mail and send it to my private account. Then I read the e-mail at home and put the data onto my tablet computer." Said Malcolm, calmer now.

"And Steve said that was OK did he?

"I didn't bother to ask because I was only using the same system as we use for sending our video clips."

Paul was horrified. He realised that Malcolm must have been e-mailing the Excel Spreadsheets to his home accounts as attachments.

"Let me understand the process that Steve set up. You take the data from the accounting system, right?"

"You, or rather the system puts out a file in Microsoft EXCEL format." Malcolm stated flatly.

"Then the file is on your work pc and you log-off the accounting system. You then log-on to the main servers and take the Excel file and attach it to an e-mail. Is that right so far?"

"Yes, that's it."

"Then you send the e-mail so that you can collect the e-mail from home and read the attachment. Now tell me, when you log-on from home and open the e-mail, you provide a password before you can open the attachment?"

"Yes, of course I do, and I enter a password when I start up the e-mail system." What's the problem?"

"Well there seem to be a number of problems. First you are sending the accounting data in clear. Oh, one other thing, do you keep the e-mails that you sent?"

"No I don't. I delete them. Steve said I had to delete the e-mails or they would be a security risk."

Paul thought for a moment. He had to think like Malcolm, there was no point thinking like an IT professional. "Tell me, if an e-mail didn't arrive at home, what would you do?"

"I'd re-send it of course. Or at least I would the next day."

"What I mean is this. Would you have to extract the accounting data again?"

"No! I realised that there could be a problem. When Steve showed me how to do the extract I realised that if I re-extracted the data the next day, I would have another day's data in there. What I do is to attach the data to an e-mail and save the original file onto my office computer. Then if there is a problem, I still have the data to re-send."

They both realised what Malcolm had said at about the same time.

"You realise that this means that the hackers have definitely been into your office computer. They have read everything you have in there."

Malcolm went very, very pale. So much so that Paul thought he was about to faint. "Are you alright?" He asked with genuine concern.

"They have the lot. They will have seen everything!" Malcolm was clearly close to hysteria.

"We have a meeting tomorrow. Before then I need to understand exactly what they have obtained. You need to check what they can have found in your computer. Or would you like me to check?"

"NO!" Malcolm blurted out. "I can do that. You have enough to do. You leave my computer to me. I'll make a full list of everything."

At least that was one thing Paul didn't have to worry about. He really did have enough on his plate. He needed to check what other e-mails could have been intercepted and who else had left their office computer turned on.

This was like fighting the great fire of London with an extremely small bucket. At least they could start to draw a line in the sand at the meeting tomorrow. He knew that he had to think carefully. He also knew that he had one potential ace up his sleeve. He was the only person in the company to know about the porn attachments that Malcolm had sent. It would be nice to have something over him, at least he could have one ally in the meeting. Let's face it, the rest of the board would be after his blood.

Chapter 8

Paul sat in his office looking out of the window and thinking about the task in hand.

He was aware that many of the staff of ASW were restless, there were the usual tell-tale signs. Earlier that morning he had heard a member of staff refer to the day as "Friday-eve" instead of "Thursday". She was wishing the week (and to some extent the company) away. The lunchtime drinks were taking a little longer and getting more frequent. He realised that the IT staff weren't having a month-end drink but a Friday drink. He had also noticed that many sales meetings were ending with a long drinking session in one of the City pubs rather than a meal and a glass of wine at a local restaurant. The signs were there for all to see. And people were definitely seeing the signs, and the people that noticed weren't just inside ASW. They were beginning to get a reputation. Nothing irreversible as yet but these things like that can have a habit of getting out of control.

Paul looked at the folder on his desk. It contained the long, technical and somewhat damming report from Laura but there was also a note by way of a separate appendix. It explained that their investigation had found a reply to a survey that Steve had completed. The answers were designed to be high level and not the sort of thing that would cause alarm but there were two questions that Steve should have thought about before answering. First was a question about the length of the password for the person answering the questionnaire. The second question asked if the company forced the use of complex passwords. Steve had answered "9" to the first and "no" to the second. Laura had checked the address of the web-site asking the questions and had found that the web-site had a .CO.UK address but was based in Russia. Steve hadn't checked that the questionnaire was from a legitimate company but even so, he should not have answered the "password length" question.

The second question was even worse, since he confirmed that his company didn't force the use of complex passwords. Generally if the company didn't force complex passwords, most would be simple lower-case letters. As the hackers (and Laura was sure the questionnaire had been from the hackers) knew Steve used 9 characters, they wouldn't need to try any shorter or longer passwords for him. The password crackers that the hackers would have available to them would probably recover his password in a reasonable time. Because Steve had died Laura didn't put the fact of the password crack in the main report, partly because it was academic, the hackers would have either cracked Steve's password or bypassed it. It was simpler to use his account but there would always have been a plan "B".

The more damning finding in the main report and this concerned the way that the hackers had managed to get through the Firewall. The truth was...they didn't. They had simply attacked the web-site and even though it didn't trade, it was still connected to their main servers and it had a "comments" area where people could leave feedback or ask questions. The fields that they would use had no content validation on them, so were open to having system commands put in and these commands would be passed through to the backend server. The hacker had simply used the web-site to mount a SQL injection attack. Once in he had been able to copy out the password file.

The report pointed out that by telling them just 2 facts about his password, it had meant that they had cracked his password very quickly. It had been a real shock to him. He read it with unease and realised that it told the truth, even if the truth was something he didn't want to hear.

However, Laura pointed out that they had allowed some suppliers to connect to their main network as an efficiency measure but ASW had not checked the security of these suppliers, so there may well be further holed into their network waiting to be discovered. He had called Laura in because he respected her experience, her frankness and most of all, her honesty. Now he was reading the result of that honesty and it wasn't enjoyable. He stared at the stark white sheets of paper. They seemed to glare back in the morning sunlight. They seemed to be particularly harsh sheets of paper as if Laura had used a special brilliant white paper for the report. Paper that would reflect the stark reality of the words inside. Yet the words were not of Laura's making, they were simply descriptive of her findings. They just told what she had found when she audited the systems. The holes in the security and the patches that should have been applied but for some reason or another had not been added to the system. It went on to describe the hardening process and the many updates and modules that had been applied, the reconfiguration of the firewalls and the many changes made to the IDS settings.

Then Laura rounded off the Management Section of the report with a long section that succinctly outlined the conversation they had regarding ASW's options. This included a series of management recommendations that applied to risk analysis, setting of standards and policy and the monitoring and auditing of ASW's IT systems. Her main message was that they should treat the security and integrity of the systems as a process and not as a single event. She pointed out that they should be following the government's '10 steps to cyber security' to protect their systems and the OWASP guide for security web development as well as checking the security of their trusted suppliers.

Laura had made it clear that she was not inviting any editorial comment. She reported what she believed to be the truth and she sent the report to Paul on the understanding that it was not doctored in any way before it was presented to the main directors of the company.

Laura has been asked on many occasions to change a report after delivery so that the "offender" could be put in a better light with the main board. She had always refused. She delivered a report on the understanding that it was distributed in its entirety and any receiving party could contact Laura to authenticate the entire contents. Of course she was not responsible if it was misreported, but if she learned of any occasion when her report was rewritten then she would expose the whole thing. It was for this reason that her report was heat bound, contained the page numbers on the header and footer and was printed double-sided . Only two copies were delivered by courier to the customer and the one electronic copy that existed was encrypted and kept on a secure stand alone server in Laura's well protected office.

The problem was that the issues were so varied and so deep-rooted that Paul knew he didn't stand a chance of addressing all but the most serious ones. Even then he would have to be fairly inventive when he reported to the board. He would need all his linguistic skills in order to convince them that he was on top of the situation. He looked at the summary findings again. The thing that was worrying Paul was the fact that Laura was absolutely convinced that ASW would find itself in the same situation again, even if it managed to ride out this particular crisis.

Of all the issues raised the most damning was embedded in a single sentence. Paul looked at the report and realised that this was not just an ASW problem, it was IT wide. During the 1970's, 80's and the beginning of the 90's the IT industry was stable. It was frantically short of staff but anyone working in IT could be sure of a secure future. Even if the rest of industry went into recession, IT seemed to be immune, or even prosper. All through the 70's and most of the 80's, the major costs in IT were hardware. The cost of the people needed to design and run the systems was much lower than the costs of the machinery. Even when the salaries were astronomic, the hardware costs eclipsed them.

With the invention of the personal computer, the PC, the various components used in IT began to be seriously mass-produced. As a result, the costs started to fall. Of course, none of this mattered to the IT professional since the early personal machines were a joke. They were slow, had pathetic memory and minimal storage. The storage that they did have was agonisingly slow when reading or writing any large file. In short, the early machines were toys. What they did have was good displays. They had sexy graphical user interfaces – (GUIs). The old-fashioned mainframes were fast but had display screens that had been designed back in the 60's and were never updated. They were OK for computer operators and programmers to use but they were completely useless for the 'real' users or worse still, the general public. As a result there was a real need to marry the technology of the PC with the mainframe.

However, the technology used on the mainframe systems was remarkably stable. If you learned to program on a mainframe, the same language would be used for ten or twenty years. Even when it was updated, it tended to be an organic growth. In other words, a program that had worked in the 70's would still run 20 years later in the 90's, in fact a large number of old COBOL programs that had been written for the Government back in the 1970s and 80s were still being used after the new millennium. The problem that the UK Government faced was the lack of COBOL programmers, most of them had retired and no-one was training in these old programming languages.

All that ended with the software written for the PC. The early DOS programs wouldn't run on Windows 3.1, so they were replaced. Then came Windows 95 and the programs were thrown out again, then windows 98 or NT and then XP and so it went on. Each time the operating system was replaced, many of the old programs needed to be replaced or have massive upgrades. And what did the PC industry do about this state of affairs? Did they apologise to their customers for causing them so much unnecessary expense? No, they simply started to refer to systems as being 'Legacy' as if it was bad. Of course, having your own unique systems would be a legacy of the investment that the company had put into IT yet the salesmen and women managed to make things sound bad. They managed to fool people into thinking that a legacy system was something that should be replaced. The end result of this thinking would be that every company in any given market sector would be running on identical software. The thing that had made the various companies different from each other would be thrown away.

Fortunately, some of the larger companies noticed what was going on but many firms continued down the road to ever more system upgrades and ever more software purchases. System life was being measured in months or at the most a few years. The IT staff found that they were in a vicious cycle themselves. The products that they worked on had such short lives that people found they were having trouble finding jobs if they were out of date. People could get out of date in a really short time.

Every time there was a new release of operating system software, or a major new database system, the IT staff argued that the company needed to have the latest software. To run the latest software they had to have the latest hardware. None of this was really for the benefit of ASW but because the staff couldn't afford to get out of date. It was the staff who needed the latest hardware and software. In short the company was being CV driven. The people in IT were so afraid of getting out of date and being unemployable that the company was spending thousands and thousands of pounds for no direct business benefit.

Paul read the phrase again. **"ASW has been CV led at the expense of the needs of the company."** What a terrible indictment of the IT team. What a terrible indictment of him. It was his job to ensure that the company remained up to date, but also to ensure that they got the best out of the IT spend. Clearly it had been wasting a large proportion of its IT budget. Worse than that, it had been as a result of getting the latest in operating systems software that the hackers had been able to get in. If they had been using an older operating system, they would have been running a system that had been thoroughly tested. If they had been checking the security of their suppliers and ensured that the input fields on their web-site were validated, they would have prevented some major holes in their security from sitting there, waiting to be exploited. They would be running a system with most of the holes patched. The hackers would have been hard pressed to find a way in. Because they were running the latest operating system, the hackers had been able to try the latest exploits and found that ASW had not yet tested and applied the latest patches. They were vulnerable.

There was another side to the coin. With the increase in the staff costs as a proportion of the IT budget many IT managers were squeezing the development times as a way of saving money. Paul realised that he was a guilty as the next manager. He was pushing the staff to deliver new developments in ever shorter times. Yet the fact that they were on the constant upgrade path meant that there were so many new systems to be put in that the staff were under constant pressure and the pressure was beginning to have serious side effects. Not only were they cutting corners but they were actually starting to lie about what was happening. If he asked his IT staff if something had been done, they would almost always answer "Yes" even when he was sure that a job hadn't been completed.

Staff realised that no matter what they did the company always seemed to demand more. Yet the IT staff themselves were responsible for a large proportion of the upgrades by needing to keep their CVs up to date in case things at ASW got intolerable. He seemed to suddenly see a whole nest of vicious circles within vicious circles. Because the IT staff were defensive about their skills, they were putting in more upgrades to the hardware and the software. Because of the number of upgrades, Paul was hammering the time-scale of each project. Because of the contracted time-scale, the projects were not being fully implemented and corners were being cut. This, in turn meant that the hackers were able to find numerous holes in their security and walk into their systems.

Paul started to read the report again. He knew that somehow he had to break the destructive cycle that many companies found themselves in. Yet he also realised that it wasn't an ASW problem so much as an IT issue. Because there were so many companies doing the same thing, he would find it hard to be in a minority of companies who were refusing to upgrade simply because the technology was there.

After informing Laura of his intentions, Paul had re-read the report in its entirety. Then after the tempestuous meeting with Malcolm he called a brief meeting of the board and informed them of the hack.

During this meeting he was deliberately curt and official. He told them that it was his unhappy duty to report that the ASW systems had been hacked and the event had been discovered shortly before Steve's death. The mix of reactions confirmed their different understandings of the concept of hacking and there were many questions. However, Paul merely confirmed that it had been discovered and that all of the holes in their network had been closed and it could not happen again. He then distributed Laura's report for them to read and digest and arranged for a full meeting and de-brief at the earliest convenient day, which was today.

He had not spoken to Malcolm at all since he left his office and he had glanced back at him as he closed his door. Malcolm always liked his door closed, he said it was more confidential and as FD he needed his privacy. Malcolm also kept his desk facing the door and his PC high-resolution screen facing away from the door and window so that it could not be seen by prying eyes. Paul wondered why he needed to have such "privacy", why was it that he always seemed to switch screens or even turn off his monitor whenever he walked into his office.

At least the images that Malcolm had sent were "legal pornography" of the type that existed in the magazines and on web-sites in the UK and USA, even if they were undesirable in the workplace they should not have a long lasting effect on the reputation of ASW. Sure, some of the older clients would have been shocked, but most would soon forget about it. Even given Malcolm's age and the fact that being Gay was a criminal offence when he was young, Paul did wonder why he was so afraid of him seeing the images on his computer. Surely that would be the only reason for him being so protective about the content of his computer, the only reason why he had insisted that he and he alone be allowed to check his own computer.

Paul looked at the clock on his desk and saw that it was nearly 10:00 and he stood and prepared himself to walk into the lion's den.

When Paul walked in Seb's office, Seb and Malcolm were already seated at opposite ends of the long oval table. Great, thought Paul – in the middle! June arrived and sat opposite Paul, giving him a cheerful smile. He liked June and found her easy to get on with, someone he could open up to, in short, an ideal HR manager.

Paul expected Seb to start the proceedings but then Bill walked in apologised for holding things up and sat next to June.

Seb must have seen the look on the others faces and explained.

"I have asked Bill to join us. He has read the report and I would like him to sit in and lend us the weight of his considerable business and IT experience in this matter"

It was said in a way that invited no argument or complaint and Seb looked directly at Paul and smiled. Bill had been at ASW for a number of years and it was plain that Seb liked and trusted him. Also Bill gave him no reason to suspect that he was anything else other than a loyal and well-respected member of IT who did a good job. Paul found him old-fashioned and set in his ways but at times he often surprised Paul with his perception and understanding of complex systems or development problems.

"Fine" said Paul and smiled at Bill. He really did not object but was a little uneasy about it.

June Smiled at Bill and said nothing and Malcolm just sat there on the edge of the chair so that his feet were planted firmly on the floor and stared ahead at Seb. So far he had avoided looking directly at Paul.

"OK – let's start" said Seb.

"Before we get down to the reason for this meeting I would like us all to be very aware that we are about to discuss events that concern Steve Jones" He looked at each in turn to emphasise the point.

"The reason we are meeting is to investigate the security breach, what actions to take and learn any lessons. I am sure that everyone at ASW has contributed to that in some way and I would like to take this opportunity to pay my respects to the memory of Steve who worked so hard to provide and maintain the IT systems at ASW. Could I propose a short silence in his memory?"

A silence fell on the table and each had their own thoughts. Paul sat there thinking – You wily old fox Seb. What a great way to say "do not blame or speak ill of the dead" well done.

Seb broke that silence. "I have read the report from Laura and while I do not fully understand all of the technical terms and references I fully comprehend the management summary and conclusions. Let me test my understanding of this by outlining the situation as I see it."

Seb looked at Paul and smiled his little apologetic smile that he used when he was being a self-deprecating about all things technical. Paul knew that Seb understood a lot more than he let on and sat back listening.

"Some six weeks ago a hacker broke into our system via a known hole in our web server and then captured a password database. This was "cracked", as you put it, and all of the major passwords were discovered. Because the userids and passwords were the same on every server, and indeed the passwords used were easy to guess, presumably because the individuals concerned chose words that were easy to remember, including" – he looked at June – "the password of PASSWORD, they could gain entry into all of our systems that were interconnected."

Seb took a sip of water and continued.

"Any perimeter security or detection systems that were in place were either bypassed or had their configuration altered so that this particular attack was not further detected or reported on, and from then on they could exist inside our small system at will for a period of time and look at any data that was kept on that network. Including" He stopped and looked around the room for effect "any PC that was left powered on overnight either with the Screensaver active or just logged off.

They also had access to the mail server and could read any e-mail, personal or business, that was stored there and any associated attachment that was stored on a personal folder.

Finally they would have had access to the creative media suit that stores the future business presentations etc. but that is protected to a degree by the client software that is used on the user's workstations. And I am assured by Roland that his people turn off their PC's every night and adopt a strict procedure to isolate and code name all client detail. – Thank heavens for that! Also I am so glad I insisted that the accounts system was kept isolated on its own network, despite the pressure I was under to integrate it!"

There was a silence around the table and Paul looked at Malcolm for the first time. "Well" he said quietly "It's not quite that simple",

Malcolm went red and shifted in his chair. He thought about sitting back but needed to keep very still and not let his posture be affected by swinging legs. Paul kept on looking at Malcolm and the unasked question was there – do you tell them or shall I?

Malcolm looked at Seb and opened his mouth.

"I have to admit that I have been working on the accounts at home in the form of an Excel spreadsheet. I have been exporting the data from the accounts systems and I then e-mail an encrypted attachment to my Hotmail account at home"

"Oh great" said Bill who immediately knew the implication of that.

Malcolm shot him a look and blurted out. "Look there was no procedure or instructions in place to cover this, I had to meet a deadline and when I asked Steve he told me how to do it – it's his fault!"

There was a long silence and Malcolm looked down at the desk aware of what he had said and done.

"I, err, I mean I, look that wasn't what I meant, I am not trying to lay blame here, but I needed to work at home and Steve showed me how Roland's people e-mailed a video clip to a client so I copied that"

It was Seb this time that swore. "Bloody hell, do you mean we have stored the accounts information on your own PC in a form that could be read and the client data on the mail server and these have possibly been taken?"

Paul looked at Malcolm and felt a pang of sympathy and regret. "Look here, it's true we don't have the correct procedures or instructions in place to handle e-mail, attachments or security of data, it's all there in the report and it's something I have to put into place. We have identified several places where we have fallen down badly. Malcolm needed to work at home and sent the spreadsheets by e-mail. He password protected them and then deleted them from his e-mail folder"

Paul did not mention Malcolm's PC or any of the data it contained.

"Also" he continued, "we have been doing the same thing with the client stuff and we also encrypted that. What we have to remember here is that we did these things to be able to do our job and make this company more prosperous. Nobody deliberately did anything that they knew would compromise the company or our clients, this is a position that we have found ourselves in because I have not put the correct procedures into place that we could all follow."

He picked up his copy of the report from Laura. "Laura makes the point very forcibly in here about that. She says that people need to choose passwords and look after the company data in the same way that they look after their personal data, pin codes, wallets etc."

"Having said that, some of the advice that we have given out regarding the use of password and switching off PC's have been ignored. It's the way people are"

"Look here people" interrupted Seb, "This is not a witch hunt or a trial. We have had a problem and we have to learn from it. When you're on the Titanic your highest priority is not 'who hit the iceberg?' it's 'where are the lifeboats'. Everybody that works here has shown incredible loyalty and commitment, including poor Steve who was killed rushing back here to address this problem, so let's take a breath and continue."

"OK" he continued "So some accounting data in the form of a spreadsheet and some client videos that existed on the main server for a short time may also be compromised" Seb looked across at Bill who was watching the series of exchanges with interest.

"Bill will you talk to Malcolm and Roland's people offline and try to ascertain exactly what data might have been seen by the hacker and report back. I need some kind of possible damage assessment. It won't help us other than to guess the worst."

Bill nodded and made a note. He looked at Malcolm "I may need access to the spreadsheets you keep at home and talk to you about how you mailed them!"

Malcolm narrowed his eyes and was about to complain but bit his lip and simply said "Sure Bill – no problem" He made a mental note to download the Evidence Eraser program that one of his Internet friends who shared his "Hobby" recommended to him. He would have to clean his disk at work completely. Home – now that was a different matter, so much stuff to get rid of but there was some material that he really did need to keep.

"Paul, I understand that the hackers gained access by hacking into a supplier and then tunnelling through into us. I don't fully understand how that works but have we blocked that particular hole?"

"Yes, we called the supplier and have removed their access to our systems. For now we are using encrypted e-mail attachments to send information to them. The e-mails are encrypted and the attachments are further protected."

"Good, before we go any further, do we have any evidence at all that any of this data has actually been copied or stolen? Do we know if it does in fact exist outside of our own organisation?"

It was a good question and one that Paul had asked himself many times. The fact was they did not know who did it or what they had seen. Yes it could be assumed by himself and Laura that because only one or two pieces of evidence had been found that nothing had been stolen but that was a bit like finding your car missing from outside your house and discovering it on next doors driveway, unmarked, undamaged and in perfect condition. There is no proof that it has been driven further than just across the driveway but it is likely that it has done many miles and been used by either a professional criminal or someone who has the keys.

"Well I can tell you what we do know. One of June's e-mails has been read by someone other than herself, we know that because of the receipt I got back on that Monday morning. We also know that several user accounts had been set up and used to modify some systems files and replace one program in particular that produced a file that reported on all userid and password use." He suspected that a rival has seen our accounting data but for now he and Malcolm were keeping that to themselves, there was no proof that the hacker had passed this on to WILLIS and SPACH, they could have got the information from a number of sources. "Now these could be the only things he has done and if that is the case he will try to get back in later. We can remove the accounts he has defined and also plug the original entry point".

Paul deliberately followed Seb's lead in using a singular expression for the hacker. It was better they thought of this as a "he" rather than "they". It minimised the impact.

"But the fact is people, that we have no evidence one way or the other that any of the information has been compromised or misused – we may find that we have just been looked at and passed over. We may have had a near miss."

"Yes Paul," said Seb "Though strictly speaking, if you nearly mess something, you hit it! But don't let's get bogged down in semantics."

Paul was very happy with the conversation so far. He was not going to tell them that both he and Laura were sure that the whole place had been gone over by a professional team and the only way they had been discovered was by being sloppy over one e-mail that was looked at. To disclose that would serve no purpose other than to put him further on the defensive with nothing to defend himself with.

Bill leaned forward "I guess time will tell!" he said and looked at Paul.

"How?" asked Seb to the table?

"Well – in my experience" it was a favourite expression of Bill's, and he did have a lot of experience in IT. "We don't know what they have, but let's assume they have everything we have. That in itself is not a problem – it's how they use it that causes us the problem"

Malcolm listened very carefully and hoped that Paul was not looking at him. "Oh shit," he thought, they might already be starting to use it!

Bill continued "If we hear nothing more we can assume that it was a Script Kiddie who was playing" He looked at the puzzled faces around the table. "A script kiddie is what the hacking profession call an inexperienced would-be-hacker that loads down some software from the Internet and uses it to trawl through many sites looking for a simple vulnerability. Once found he exploits it as far as he can and then moves on to the next site. It is arguable that he would not know what to do with the vast amount of information available and would probably be just joy-riding."

Paul was impressed. Laura had said something similar and the fact that Bill was knowledgeable in this made him feel both comfortable that Bill was an ally but fearful that he would see right through Paul's defence.

"If, on the other hand, things start to happen then we can assume that someone wanted to hack us to use the information. As a general rule, the more time goes by and nothing happens – the safer we are, but there are exceptions. If a criminal steals credit card data they will often wait for several months before using what they have taken because when a victim has their credit or debit card used, they will invariably try to work out where it was stolen from. To do this they will normally think of the last time they used it and blame 'that' company. By leaving things for a few months it is very hard to work out which actual company was the cause of the theft. In our case the data will be of commercial value and that will reduce rapidly with time, so we can be fairly sure that if they use the data quickly, then the motive behind the hack was purely criminal. One possible scenario is he might contact us and ask for a ransom. Of course if we pay it we have no real proof or evidence that he will not sell it on anyway. If we find that the information hasn't been used for a month or two, then it is more likely that the hack was the work of a teenager who simply wanted to break into our systems or a criminal who is after personal data."

There was another long silence during which each of the members was lost in their own thoughts.

"So to summarise the situation – we know we have been hacked and there has been minimal actual damage. We also know that most of our corporate data could have been seen but we don't know that it **has** been seen. We have closed all of the holes and checked all of our contentious areas such as web-site and sent e-mails and nothing has been done that we think could damage our brand or image. After the event we have now closed all of the holes." Seb looked around the table. "Have we left anything out or is there anything else I need to know?"

Paul also looked around the table and let his gaze fall on Malcolm. His gaze was returned with a defiant stare. Nobody said anything.

"OK" continued Seb – "what lessons do we have to learn here because this must never happen again."

It was Bill who spoke first. "I read the report with some interest. I must congratulate you Paul on choosing Laura, she is very good, very experienced. The section where she deals with this being an industry problem is absolutely bang on"

Paul smiled at the Bill type expression. He let him continue.

"Back in the late seventies and early eighties we did get things right and although the systems were a bit clunky and not what you call GUI, they worked and were manageable. The biggest problem we had then was capacity management where the demand for processing outstripped the ability to deliver it so we managed to contain costs by optimisation and tuning. Now processing power is in abundance and even the simplest of people, even the hacker who attacked us, probably has more power than I used to manage back in 1973 when I was Data Centre Manager at UK Petroleum. That's how he cracked the encrypted passwords no doubt.

But we did get a lot right then and we did manage the systems and ensure that the user was serviced and data integrity was maintained"

Bill looked at Paul and answered his next question before Paul asked it. "No Paul I am not advocating that we buy a mainframe. Simply that we take a look at what we are trying to do here at ASW and deliver the IT set-up that suits us, not one that suits your staff!"

"Oh come on Bill" Paul was getting a bit heated now, "I didn't choose this set-up, you know that, it was here before I arrived"

"No but you let it develop and hired in the young guys straight out of university who knew nothing about data integrity. They just wanted to use the new software, new hardware and play with their new toys" Responded Bill.

He continued. "Look I really liked Steve, he was a nice guy but he never wanted to listen when we had a security or backup issue. Yes he wanted to deliver the systems to the users but he was only really interested in his own CV. I tried to warn you many times Seb" Bill was looking at Seb now. "Every time a new system came in, every time we had to upgrade nobody ever thought about recovery times, backups, system tests, disaster recovery test or any kind of risk analysis that revolved around data integrity.

When I suggested a Penetration Test be performed by an outside agency on our network and web-site" He looked at Paul now "You took it personally and accused me of trying to undermine you. In the end Seb, you said we couldn't afford it. Now it seems we couldn't afford not to!"

He let the words hang in the air. Seb looked across at Bill. "Yes I have read the report too Bill and I have to say I agree with you" Looking at Paul, Seb continued

"I am not going to lay blame on you or Steve or anyone in this company. What has happened is an outside event. Someone hacked us because they could"

"June" Seb looked at his HR director. "You have been very quiet, do you have any comment."

June smiled and thought for a moment "Do you mean other than saying sorry I chose a simple password? No. I don't use my personal e-mail or systems for anything other than correspondence to employment agencies or head-hunters. Also most of my information is kept in the folders on my PC and consists of CV's etc. I doubt if that is of any use to a hacker. However one cannot be sure.

I tend to agree with Bill, but I can understand the issue Paul has with hiring the right staff – after all I helped him do that.

I think it would be a good use of our skills and our investment in people to sit back and think about the type of IT systems that we want to use. I am very concerned about the disciplinary issues that arise from the incorrect use of the Internet, computer games and even playing with the colours on the PC.

Oh and we do need to ensure that there is a suitable training program to raise awareness over security issues, maybe even build something about maintaining security into employees contracts. Other than that – nothing else to say"

As usual June managed to inject a note of real common sense into the conversation and Seb looked at her in admiration.

"Right" he said drawing a line in the conversation "This is what we are going to do"

"It seems to me that we have fallen into the trap of relying on the technology of our systems and forgetting the well tried and tested principles that have been running our lives for years. I took no comfort from reading the report on Steve's death that the car we supplied him as part of his employment package worked exactly as it was designed and maybe contributed towards his death. In a similar way we have allowed ourselves to be persuaded to rely on new technology and systems to run our business and completely abdicated ourselves from any responsibility in managing them.

I want to take a step back and review exactly how we run our IT and make the technology work for us rather than letting it drive our actions and decisions" Seb paused.

"Paul, I took the liberty of calling Laura in for a meeting with Bill and me, and before you say anything I asked her to keep the meeting confidential, and judging from your expression, I see she did. I was interested to see who we had hired to check out our systems. I have to say that choosing her was a very good decision, she was confident and clearly knew her subject very well, so I have full confidence in her findings. I would like to hire her but I fear that a: we can't afford to and b: even if we could, she would find life here to be too limiting. However, I want to use her expertise to help us."

He glanced around the room. Paul would have expected Seb to be 'old school' and possibly quite sexist but it seems that he was shrewd enough to know when he was talking to an expert and age, colour or gender were not important if the well being of the company was at stake.

"Paul – I want you to hire one of Laura's people for a short contract and make sure that our systems are fully hardened and as impervious to attack as possible. I also want them to recommend the immediate steps we need to take to ensure we have the correct procedures in place to stop any type of business compromise caused by incorrect use of e-mail, copying data, password use, access to incorrect data or applications and the use of our PC's. Also I want you to start the process of defining a Full Data Security Policy that encompasses all of the lessons we have learnt so far. You have been on enough seminars and courses – let's see a return from them"

"Bill – I want you to look at the use of our IT systems from a different point of view. What steps do we need to take to start delivering IT systems that the business needs, even if some of the results aren't what it wants. We all know that the Marketing Department want to use their home computers tablets and phones for work but I don't want to introduce any new vulnerabilities. If we are to let any staff use their own equipment it must be on the basis of accessing a secure area in the network and not having company data on their own devices."

Seb continued. "Then I want you to research how our competitors and similar business models use their IT infrastructure. If there are any lessons to be learned or a simpler and less complicated business approach to IT, I want to know about it! I will give you a clue here Bill, last month I was at a business lunch and met an IT Director who told me a story about Cromwell Insurance. Over drinks we were talking about investment in web-sites. He related to me that they deliberately downsized their investment in new web applications. Yet at the same time they completely revamped the security surrounding their applications and installed a Data Loss Prevention program to protect the intellectual property and the customer data that they were storing. This was at a time when the vogue was to inform the stock market of the large amounts invested in web technology. He said that Cromwell had decided to consolidate their main IT systems and ensure that they were well protected before looking at an upgrade".

"And one final thing", Seb continued looking at Paul, then Bill. "Cromwell have also accredited themselves against a Government Cyber scheme called Essential Security, or Essentials Cyber Controls, I can't quite remember the exact title"

"Cyber Essentials" – said Bill quickly.

"Yes – that's it" Seb continued. "Cyber Essentials is the phrase he used. They said it was an accredited scheme that helped you secure your whole I.T. environment"

He looked at Paul – "Chat this through with your expert – Laura and see if it's something we can use"

Seb looked at them all. "It goes without saying that all IT investment is on hold until we get a good handle on this".

Seb looked at June "Maybe we can cut some costs and save some jobs eh!"

"Malcolm. I want your complete co-operation in this and this means your people not being cosseted with their fancy big monitors and high resolution colour printers just to print financial graphs. Also give me a run down on the maintenance costs of our hardware and software and exactly what we pay and to whom. I am sure that we can consolidate our IT costs there by just buying and using what we really need"

Malcolm sat back in his chair and looked straight ahead - expressionless, only his alternately swinging legs giving a hint of his demeanour.

Seb looked around and wound up the meeting. "OK that's good to start with. Let's meet back here in 10 days to report. I am expecting the go-ahead from MAZOTA UK soon about the full advertising campaign and that will be a welcome boost."

"Hopefully that would lead to more work with them and others. This may just turn out to be a blessing in disguise!"

Seb stood up and pulled together his papers. As the others left the room he pulled Paul aside and said quietly.

"Paul. This is not a good time to discuss anything further, especially after Steve's death but I am really looking for you to redeem yourself here by helping me to turn this around. To be honest there are others who are after your blood and they have a good point to make. I'm not blind, I know there are troubles at home and I can see that you have done your best here, but if this thing gets any worse, then I am going to have to make an example of someone. So don't let me down any more – OK?"

Paul looked at Seb as he walked out of the room and felt his whole world shrink. He thought of Alyson, Sonia, the kids, Malcolm and his porn, the accounts data and the company's rivals. How quickly a stable, secure environment can change!

He walked down the hall to his office and decided to pack up for the day and join the others at the pub

Chapter 9

Sebastian sat at his desk on the following Monday morning. It was 08:15am and he had been in since 07:30. He wasn't really the kind of business director that was always in early and stayed late, but he had a little Monday morning ritual where he rose early, walked the dog and was scrubbed up and fed ready to catch the 06:50 into London from the affluent suburb of Bickley in Kent

His Monday Habit was to arrive at the office with a copy of the Financial Times and a Latté with a dash of Hazelnut syrup from one of the corner coffee shops that seemed to be breeding overnight in London and catch up on things financial before the round of Monday meetings.

Most of his spare time over the weekend, his morning preparations and the train ride in had been spent in thought about the meeting last Friday and the events surrounding the security violation and illegal access. Sebastian could not bring himself to easily use the word 'hack' or 'hacker'. In his opinion it glorified a process or activity that was in essence vandalism and theft and the people that perpetrated the crime were little better than pickpockets or muggers.

He felt that the meeting had gone well and the actions clearly defined. Paul had been negligent in many ways and it was obvious for some time that he had not been giving the job his full attention. The relationship he had with Alyson, Malcolm's secretary was not well known but it was obvious to Seb by the body language, reactions and general activities that something was going on. Seb had only met Sonia at the social functions and she was a bright, attractive lady who was obviously devoted to Paul and their children, but that was the way things were sometimes, the stress and pressure of working in the City could take its toll in many ways. It was Paul's business how he conducted his private life and as long as work did not suffer then Seb kept out of things.

Now however this had happened and the other directors were openly talking about Paul's obligations and responsibilities. Seb hoped that the whole situation would be resolved quickly and that no detrimental effects would surface as a result of the "hack".

In reality Seb liked Paul. He liked his approach to things and the way he treated his staff. He liked his easy manner in front of users and customers and his pragmatic approach to running IT. He was also aware, however, that Paul was guilty of exactly the things that Laura Billings had criticised in her excellent report. Paul wanted to make his name as a man that exploited the newer technologies to the full and he embraced the modern Open Systems approach to IT. Bill had said many times that some of Paul's more extravagant and controversial decisions regarding new technology would come back to bite them.

It was a good decision to involve Bill in the meeting and the resulting action and Seb had come to realise that although Bill was labelled as a dinosaur and was sometimes derided by others in the company, many of his comments and opinions were sound and based on experience and the desire for the business to use IT correctly. Bill belonged to many of the industry user groups and he had recently given a presentation about the way that IT was failing smaller companies. He believed that too many companies didn't get the basics right and that IT was too focused on itself and not the businesses that it was supposed to serve.

Bill had started in IT at the time when IBM completely monopolised the Large Systems market. Nearly all of the hardware, software, database products, and application development packages were supplied by IBM and this in itself spawned a thriving third party supplier market with companies springing up in all areas that exploited the holes left by the IBM offerings. One of the common phrase of the day was "nobody ever got fired for buying IBM" and this was true. They grew to completely monopolise the market by producing dependent hardware and software offerings that forced users to follow the upgrade and growth paths that were dictated by this monolithic company. Many senior managers at that time considered IBM an arrogant company.

In Bill's opinion many ruses and ploys were used such as the bundling together of dependent software into what was called Customer Based Installation Productivity Options. This meant that you installed everything from one installation package and from then on used and paid for what you wanted. The strategy was that many products only worked well with others in the package so that the customer was "encouraged" to use the lot, even though many of the IBM products were inferior to the third party offerings on the market. Many companies tried to go down the third party software route but this was difficult. IBM did their best to make other software difficult to integrate and tried to make hardware and operating systems features available only to "reserved" programs.

Then IBM forced their users to switch to usage based pricing, which although it was initially offered as being cheaper for the user was structured so that the user was soon sucked into using the whole package offered and the usage price was then increased.

Finally the backlash came in the form of a USA government investigation into their monopoly and business practice and rejection from the users who were looking at alternative and seemingly cheaper platforms and software – such as Microsoft.

The phrase involving "Frying-pan and Fire" kept coming to mind. Bill would remember a time when a system would be designed by a Systems Analyst, written and tested by a Programmer and run by a Production Support department who worked with the Computer Operators. There were only a handful of programming languages and the applications on the computer were completely ring-fenced by a security system that only allowed the data to be seen by authorised users. The Security Analyst could grant access but didn't automatically have access. Once the industry moved to Servers you had a situation where there was a known top level account and if you got hold of that you had access to all the data and applications on that server and any other servers that were closely linked together. "One Account to rule them all" as they may have said in Lord of the Rings.

Seb was not present at the presentation but he heard many people commenting on the session and Bill reported back that it was very well received. The real clincher was at the end when Bill ran through the whole presentation again very quickly, but he had replaced the name of IBM with Microsoft. The audience loved it and of course it was absolutely true, Microsoft was just as guilty of manipulating and forcing the market down the same path. One of completely tying in the customer and forcing out any competition.

Bill had only recently pointed out the change to the charging structure that Microsoft had introduced that centred on annual charges for usage and included automatic upgrades to their software, upgrades that were not needed and forced the user to improve or increase other areas of your infrastructure. It's as if they were all in league together.

And now of course now ill would point you to the fact that history was repeating itself yet again with the two leading companies Apple and Google. They started off with a new and fresh approach and changed the way we thought about computing only to now tie people in with architectures, suites of applications and themes and learning all the lessons about security, data integrity and resilience all over again.

It came as no surprise that Bill knew of the Cyber Essentials scheme. Yes Bill was a good asset and he needed to consult him more.

Seb's thoughts had also centred on the others. June's reactions and opinion was exactly as Seb had expected. She always took that sensible human approach and he wished that he could ensure that any cost cutting did not reflect forced redundancies. It must be soul destroying for a HR person to call in people to make them redundant after spending so much time selecting, employing and nurturing them in the first place.

Malcolm's reaction was as expected although he did seem to be much quieter than normal. There were times during the meeting when Paul was maybe open to comment or attack when Seb would have expected the acid or stinging comment from Malcolm, but he was surprisingly quiet. Perhaps Malcolm was being kind or showing some sympathy with Paul and the company situation.

So it was down to Paul to work with Laura and his people to review the current systems status and ensure that they did not suffer this type of attack again. Once that was done they would see what came out of Bill's study as to what direction they took this in.

Seb sipped his flavoured coffee and relaxed back in his chair to read the paper.

Things were not so relaxed in Malcolm's comfortable large four bedroom detached house that he shared with his mother. He had been up most of the night trying to make sense of the terrible situation he had found himself in.

It started yesterday when he went out for his usual Sunday afternoon walk in the local country park. After Lunch with his mother and helping her clear up the kitchen he would leave the house to walk to the park some 2 miles away. There he would walk round the large park and lakes on the exercise track that took in woodland walks and went past the many recreation areas, adventure playground and swings.

Occasionally he would sit on the same park bench. Near the pond and feed the ducks, maybe it was a small example of him staying in control. He chose which ones to throw the bread to and which to ignore.

He had been sitting there for some 20 minutes when one of the many roller-skaters who used the paths stopped in front of him and dropped a brown jiffy bag on his lap. He looked up to see a dark skinned man wearing a bobble hat and big dark sunglasses look away and skate off in the direction of a larger path that led to the main car park.

Malcolm looked down at the brown paper bag upon which was written his name. He looked up again after the skater and then around him at the other benches and surrounding grass. There was no-one close or watching him and he picked up the bag and felt it.

Many thoughts went through his mind, some irrational, some stupid, but he couldn't think why anyone would want to deliver a package to him in this way. Obviously someone who knew he would be here at this time!

He opened the bag and drew out a plain unmarked manila folder.

In the folder was a series of Excel spread-sheets but these didn't contain company accounts, as he had expected when he first saw them. These contained details from his work computer about a series of increasingly large investments that he had made. Investments that he didn't have the money to cover if they had gone bad and some of them had done just that.

There was enough evidence to show that whoever had sent them knew the extent of Malcolm's "Hobby". He was a good Accountant and had been talking to a few other fellow professionals about financial systems. One of them had explained that they spent their spare time "day trading" and provided you understood the markets, there was a great deal of money to be had. Malcolm had looked into the subject and it seemed fairly straight forward, all he needed was a small amount of capital and he could make some serious money. The fact was that he was good at controlling money that other people had made but he didn't understand the markets and couldn't predict which way they would move. He had lost a great deal of money. To cover this he had created a new "Supplier" account and started to pay for his losses out of company funds. Of course, once he started to make a profit he would repay the "loan" but he simply wasn't very good, so the losses continued. More than the money he had lost was the fact that he would have to admit that he was a failure and that was his greatest fear. How would he tell his mother?

Malcolm nearly fainted. His heart beat faster and faster and the sweat was bursting out of his forehead and running down his back. The full enormity of what had happened hit him. His complete PC had been accessed, investigated and files from it copied to produce these reports.

At that point when he thought it could not be any worse his mobile phone rang. He fumbled to get to the phone deep in his anorak pocket and looked at the display. "number unavailable" was being displayed. He hesitantly answered it.

The voice at the end of the phone was very monotone and slightly un-real. "Mr Shoreham – by now you will have seen the contents of the package that was just delivered to you!"

Malcolm was almost hysterical – "Who are you? What do you want? Why are you harassing me like this?" Malcolm went into overdrive quoting all of the rhetoric that people do in this situation simply to attack the other party and put off the inevitable conclusion that his activities were known by an outside party.

The voice continued. "Listen to me – very carefully" It said in a slow deliberate way. "We do not care what you do with your private life we just want your co-operation. Do you understand me?"

Malcolm was not a stupid man. He knew it wasn't an official authority that was doing this and the words gave him slight hope that the outcome was not entirely bad.

He stammered out the words. "Yes – what do you want"

The voice continued. "Next week you will be invited to vote, along with the other members of the ASW board, on a takeover bid from a rival company. Whatever the arguments or your feelings about this you will vote in favour of this. You will then receive a very fair offer from a valid agent for your complete share holding in the company – which you will accept"

Malcolm's stomach was churning now and he bent forward to put his head in his hands. "Oh my god! – Oh my God!"

"If you refuse to comply with this request, a copy of this folder along with your most recent trading statements showing that you have lost in excess of 2 million pounds of ASW's money will be sent to every member of the Board and also to the daily papers.

There was a long pause while the caller let that information sink in. "Do we understand each other?" he asked.

Malcolm was scarlet with a combination of indignation and guilt. "This is common black-mail!" He blustered.

"That's right." Said the voice calmly. "We do understand each other. We will be in touch." and the phone clicked off.

Malcolm got home later that afternoon and spent the rest of the day and all night trying to see if there was any way he could repay the money but no matter how he looked at the figures, there was no way he could clear his debt. He would have to go along with his instructions.

The next morning, after a fitful and sleepless night he called in to Alyson's voicemail and left a message that he would not be in the office due to a bad bout of food poisoning and gastric problems.

Paul on the other hand had a great weekend. After the meeting with Seb and the brief warning he had at the end he went down the pub to join the other Friday Night drinkers from ASW and maybe find Alyson.

Then he remembered that she was leaving early to spend the weekend with her parents in Bristol so he sat in a group idly chatting when Sonia called him on his mobile.

She reminded him that they were invited next door for dinner that night and the baby-sitter was due at 8:00pm. She sounded excited at the thought of getting out and he chatted with her briefly saying he was also looking forward to it and he would be home in good time.

When he got home Jake was already out at his friend's house where he was staying the night and Katie was ready for bed and watching a Simpson's video. He sat with his daughter and laughed with her at The Simpson's – although not at the same bits – while Sonia dressed. After that he went upstairs to shower. They left at just before 8:00 and went next door for a really pleasant evening with their friends and neighbours.

Paul managed to forget everything that was happening at work and after several glasses of a good South African Cabernet began to enjoy the company. Sonia was wearing a very attractive black dress that made the most of her slim body and as he sat there chatting and drinking he did something that he had not done for many years. He flirted with his wife.

When they got home that night and the sitter was paid and gone, Paul and Sonia made love for the first time in weeks and then lay talking into the small hours. Paul discussed with his wife their family; their home, her aspirations and what she wanted from life. He found himself rediscovering the woman who he had been living with for several years and who was the mother of his children.

The rest of the weekend was spent as a close family. Paul and Sonia spent all weekend together enjoying each other's company and on Sunday they took the kids to Thorpe Park, the big adventure park just off the M3.

It was a lovely weekend and just what Paul needed. Sonia was up and about when he left that morning and kissed him gently as he went out the door. Things had changed and there was a renewed intimacy in their lives. He arrived for work on Monday morning with very mixed thoughts about nearly spoiling a very good marriage, getting stuck into his job, avoiding Alyson and her questions about his weekend and, looking forward to working with Laura and her team sorting out the systems.

When Paul entered his office and he put his case down on the floor. Taking of his coat he noticed a large brown Jiffy Bag on his desk that had a TNT sticker on it. He didn't remember ordering anything from an Internet site or mail-order and he picked it up to look at the senders address. It was sent from a London address, a Regus office in Lombard Street and was delivered early Monday morning.

Curiosity got the better of him and he started to open it.

Seb was idly scanning the pink newspaper and sipping his coffee. He turned a page and noticed that it was a full-page advertisement for the new Lexda Coupe that was to be launched soon. He wanted to look closely at this as it would compete with the new ads that he was waiting to progress and he began to fold the paper to lay it out his desk when he froze.

There in big black letters, in Comic Sans large point font, at the centre of the page were the words "The drive in your life"

Seb uttered words that were totally alien to him "What the Hell is happening here!" He simply could not believe it. The centre point of their new Mazota car campaign that was threaded through all of the copy, billboards, TV, Cinema and Internet Ads was there in the middle of the Lexda Ad.

"Oh my god, Oh shit, shit, shit" How could they have got those words, how dare they steal their ideas, and how was he going to handle this with Brian Adams the UK boss at Mazota.

He sat there lost in it all wondering what to do next. He had not noticed his secretary arriving for work and answering the ringing phone. He looked up from his lap as she came through the adjoining door to his office.

"Seb, I have Mr Adams on the phone from Mazota, he wants to talk to you urgently!" she smiled. She guessed it was the good news from them about the campaign.

Paul sat in his chair looking at the A4 sheets of paper spread over his desk. He had opened the Jiffy Bag and the moment he looked at the contents his whole mood and demeanour had changed. In the bag were newly printed copies on sharp white A4 paper of nearly all of the e-mails that he had exchanged with Alyson in the recent past. They contained long passionate explanations of what he wanted to do to her when they were alone, short notes to confirm hotel bookings, train timetables, meeting points and many, many "I Love You" and "missing you" notes they had sent each other.

Other sheets contained copies of entries in his network diary that detailed trips over weekends and notes giving Hotel details and bookings.

Finally there were three large glossy black and white photographs that showed him and Alyson sitting at a restaurant table, together outside the restaurant getting into a taxi and finally entering the front door of Alyson's apartment block.

These were taken very recently on the last occasion when they had met. They had eaten at their favourite Italian restaurant and then gone back to her flat. Paul had left at 01:30 to drive home using an industry awards dinner as an excuse.

He sat there somewhat bewildered. What had happened? Did Sonia suspect something and hired a Private Detective to snoop on him? Why were these being sent to him, had they also been sent to his home? He picked up the phone in panic and then put it down again. As he did so it rang.

He jumped then looked at the caller ID display to see if his own number was displayed. It was blank which meant it came from a source that did not attach the caller ID. He picked up the phone and composed himself – it could be anyone on a legitimate call.

"Hello – Paul Taylor" he said in his calmest voice.

A flat and monotone voice said. "Mr Taylor, you have just received a brown envelope containing some very sensitive material relating to your relationship with an employee of ASW!" It was a statement rather than a question.

"Who the hell are you and what are you playing at!" Paul shouted down the phone. He started to panic, everything around him was beginning to spin and he was sweating. He opened his mouth to say more but the voice interrupted him in a tone that made him stop and listen.

"Mr Taylor we do not care about your personal life or what you do outside of your marriage. We want to make you an offer" The voice left a deliberate long silence hanging there while it let Paul think about what was said.

Paul's mind went through hoops. They were obviously the people that had hacked the network and captured this information. They had then used this information and organised for him to be followed and photographs taken of him. This was exactly what everyone dreaded, the action after the hack. But why use it like this?

"What kind of an offer? What have I got that you could possibly want?" Paul said weakly.

The voice on the other end listened carefully to the manner and tone of Paul's voice. His measured his words carefully. "There is about to be a takeover bid made on ASW by another company. You will vote for this takeover in any meeting of the shareholders that you attend. If the takeover is successful you will, along with others, join the newly formed company as a technical consultant along with an increase in pay. The shares you hold in ASW will form a shareholding in the new company and be worth considerably more." There was another long silence and Paul thought the voice was going to continue.

At length Paul said "And that's it?"

"Yes" was the reply.

"What about this package?" asked Paul.

"That was merely to get your attention!. We have no wish to alienate you. We just want to be sure of your co-operation" The voice softened a little and let Paul down gently.

"You see Mr Taylor, it's in your interest to participate in this matter positively. You have a lot to lose if there are any negative feelings about this"

Paul got the message loud and clear. In fact his mind was working ahead. If there was a takeover and a job was his it would be a new start in a company that would want him to keep quiet about the hack, for Christ sake - they invoked it!

"Do we have an understanding Mr Taylor?"

Paul looked out of the window at the early Monday sunshine. "Yes, I suppose we do"

"Excellent – we will be in touch with you if we need you!" The line went dead.

Paul sat there for a long time thinking about this turn of events. The human organism is genetically programmed to survive. His thoughts did not rest at all on loyalty or guilt. They centred on surviving the mess he was in with Seb and the hack and how he could dump Alyson without any fallout. Seb's last words to him on Friday meant that with any fallout from the hack he would lose his job. Here he was in the middle of major fallout and there was a way that he could not only keep his job but also find himself in a better position.

The phone rang again and he looked at the display. It was Seb so he let it ring twice more and picked it up to speak in a clear, calm voice. "Hello" he said in a gentle tone.

"Paul, Its Seb here. Get to my office immediately – we have a major problem with the Mazota account."

Paul was about to ask what kind of problem but the phone clicked off. He rose from his desk and walked out of his office.

Chapter 10

Paul drove his Mercedes into the ASW car park and looked around. Many of the older cars that he used to park alongside were missing. Malcolm's Volvo had not been parked here since the Friday of the management meeting after the Hack. In fact he had never returned to work, having been ill for two weeks then signalling his vote on the takeover by letter. Then he had sold his shares in the company and resigned.

Paul had in fact tried to call Malcolm's home during that period for his advice on shares and investments. Although they did not like each other – Paul considered Malcolm to be a financial wizard and had asked him for advice from time to time. On calling Paul had been told that Malcolm was abroad on an extended holiday. Good for him. He did not really like him but he is at least now going to relax and enjoy his money.

June's BMW was there, and probably had been there since 7:00am. As the HR director of WILLIS & SPACH she had a lot to do in ensuring that job integration worked seamlessly and no redundancies were made.

Roland's space was empty and would be until about 10:30. His new Jaguar would zoom in and take its spot, he would jump out and swagger into the office to command his expanded creative team and work on the Mazota and Lexda accounts.

Bill's old space was taken by the new Security Manager's BMW. This car had also been there since 8:00am as he had much to do in setting policy and ensuring that the security and data integrity process was always a high priority and the new policy was strictly adhered to. Bill had taken the generous redundancy that was on offer and had retired to the country. He would no doubt pop up again at user groups and be quoted in articles written for the computer press.

The pride of place in the car park, the space that used to belong to Seb, was taken by a beautiful classic Jaguar that was owned by the Managing Director of WILLIS & SPACH. He had wasted no time in moving his key staff into the ASW offices and using their superior premises, IT systems and Creative Talents to enthusiastically launch his bid to become the most prestigious Ad Agency in the City.

Paul sat there looking around him and thought of the last few months. He thought – You Never Know! He left his car and went into reception. He had an appointment with HR and he was a few minutes early. His car was five years old and older than the other cars around him, but then he was no longer driving a company car and he was only there to collect his personal belongings, he had been the first casualty of the hack and the take-over.

The meeting when the takeover bid was accepted by the team was a quick and sombre affair. Each avoided the others eyes and apart from a couple of curt comments from Seb it passed without incident.

That was in stark contrast to the meeting 3 days earlier when Brian Admonson of Mazota sat in Sebs office and accused the whole company of incompetence, criminal negligence and almost industrial espionage. He was absolutely livid that the strap line for his campaign has been used at the eleventh hour by Lexda.

Eventually the truth came out and after hearing of the hack he walked out vowing never to deal with ASW again and threatening to sue for all of the money lost and for the cost of a new campaign at a rival agency. In fact he would have taken his account abroad if it had not been for Roland who took him to lunch and offered the services of WILLIS & SPACH almost free of charge in exchange for his silence on the matter. The end result was that the campaign was launched in its entirety with everything the same except for a very different slogan. It was currently very successful.

As Paul walked through the main office he passed Alyson's empty desk outside Malcolm's old office. Alyson had been offered another post in the New York office of WILLIS & SPACH. It was a good move for her and he wished her well. In fact she did not take much persuasion. She knew it would never have worked with Paul but it was fun while it lasted, and there was a particularly cute Account Manager in the NY office that she had met at a Social event in London. He had said his goodbyes to Alyson on a wet Wednesday evening outside her flat and he had gone home to Sonia.

Things with Paul's family could not be better. Sonia was pleased that Paul was paying her more attention and assumed that it was as a result of him losing his job. For her part she had been accepted for a part time course at the local Art College.

He walked past his old office and looked at the desk. Silly really but he felt relieved when it did not contain a brown Jiffy Bag.

His thoughts briefly went to the hack again. It could never be proved of course that it was a paid act of espionage, although with hindsight being an exact science, it did fit with all of the events to assume that WILLIS & SPACH commissioned the hack to find any dirt on ASW. They could never have known that they would find enough to manoeuvre or encourage a hostile takeover.

In any event – he had a generous settlement in exchange for his silence and a cast iron reference so he was not unduly concerned. However he was older and wiser, and indeed happier than he had been for a long while and life would now be much different, whoever he ended up working for.

Part 2

Advice from HMG

The following document is from www.CPNI.Gov.UK and contains advice to companies about how to secure their Cyber resources. While the document is designed to work for all companies some of the advice will be more applicable to larger organisations. However, there is much that is worth reading and it will provide helpful advice as your company grows. It is always worth checking for the latest advice from the government by looking at www.CPNI.Gov.UK regularly.

We print the government 10 steps in full and then in summary to see why ASW was vulnerable to attack. If you find that you don't know how to implement the advice, then you can contact your local Cyber Security Cluster www.ukcybersecurityforum.com who will point you at your local Cluster and they will be happy to give you guidance.

10 Steps to Cyber Security:
Step 1 - Information Risk Management Regime

Detailed cyber security information and advice concerning your organisation's information risk management regime.

Summary

It is best practice for an organisation to apply the same degree of rigour to assessing the risks to its information assets as it would to legal, regulatory, financial or operational risk. This can be achieved by embedding an information risk management regime across the organisation, which is actively supported by the Board, senior managers and an empowered Information Assurance (IA) governance structure. Defining and communicating the organisation's attitude and approach to risk management is crucial. Boards may wish to consider communicating their risk appetite statement and information risk management policy across the organisation to ensure that employees, contractors and suppliers are aware of the organisation's risk management boundaries.

What is the risk?

Risk is an inherent part of doing business. For any organisation to operate successfully it needs to address risk and respond proportionately and appropriately to a level which is consistent with the organisation's risk appetite. If an organisation does not identify and manage risk it can lead to business failure. A lack of effective information risk management and governance may lead to the following:

Increased exposure to risk Information risk must be owned at Board level. Without effective risk governance processes it is impossible for the Board to understand the risk exposure of the organisation. The Board must be confident that information risks are being managed within tolerance throughout the lifecycle of deployed systems or services

123

Missed business opportunities Where risk decisions are being taken at junior level without effective governance and ownership back to senior levels, it may promote an overly cautious approach to information risk which may lead to missed business opportunities. Alternatively, an overly open approach may expose the organisation to unacceptable risks

Ineffective policy implementation An organisation's Board has overall ownership of the corporate security policy. Without effective risk management and governance processes the Board will not have confidence that its stated policy is being consistently applied across the business as a whole

Poor reuse of security investment A lack of effective governance means that information risk management activities may be undertaken locally when they could be more effectively deployed at an organisational level

How can the risk be managed?

Establish a governance framework
A governance framework needs to be established that enables and supports a consistent and empowered approach to information risk management across the organisation, with ultimate responsibility for risk ownership residing at Board level.

Determine the organisation's risk appetite
Agree the level of information risk the organisation is prepared to tolerate in pursuit of its business objectives and produce a risk appetite statement to help guide information risk management decisions throughout the business.

Maintain the Board's engagement with information risk
The risks to the organisation's information assets from a cyber attack should be a regular agenda item for Board discussion. To ensure senior ownership and oversight, the risk of cyber attack should be documented in the corporate risk register and regularly reviewed; entering into knowledge sharing partnerships with other companies and law enforcement can help you in understanding new and emerging threats that might be a risk to your own business and also to share mitigations that might work.

Produce supporting policies
An overarching corporate information risk policy needs to be created and owned by the Board to help communicate and support risk management objectives, setting out the information risk management strategy for the organisation as a whole.

Adopt a lifecycle approach to information risk management
The components of a risk can change over time so a continuous through-life process needs to be adopted to ensure security controls remain appropriate to the risk.

Apply recognised standards
Consider the application of recognised sources of security management good practice, such as the ISO/IEC 27000 series of standards, and implement physical, personnel, procedural and technical measures.

Make use of endorsed assurance schemes
Consider adopting the **Cyber Essentials** Scheme. It provides guidance on the basic controls that should be put in place and offers a certification process that demonstrates your commitment to cyber risk management.
Go to www.itgovernance.co.uk/**Cyber-Essentials**

Educate users and maintain their awareness
All users have a responsibility to manage the risks to the organisation's Information and
Communications Technologies (ICT) and information assets. Provide appropriate training and user education that is relevant to their role and refresh it regularly; encourage staff to participate in knowledge sharing exchanges with peers across business and Government.

Promote a risk management culture
Risk management needs to be organisation-wide, driven by corporate governance from the top down, with user participation demonstrated at every level of the business.

10 Steps to Cyber Security:
Step 2 - Secure Configuration

Detailed cyber security information and advice concerning the secure configuration of your organisation.

Summary

By putting in place corporate policies and processes to develop secure baseline builds and manage the configuration and the ongoing functionality of all Information and Communications Technologies (ICT), organisations can greatly improve the security of their ICT systems. Good corporate practice is to develop a strategy to remove or disable unnecessary functionality from ICT systems and keep them patched against known vulnerabilities. Failure to do so is likely to result in increased exposure of the business and its ICT to threats and vulnerabilities and therefore increased risk to the confidentiality, integrity and availability of systems and information.

What is the risk?

Establishing and then actively maintaining the secure configuration of ICT systems should be seen as a key security control. ICT systems that are not locked down, hardened or patched will be particularly vulnerable to attacks that may be easily prevented.
Organisations that fail to produce and implement corporate security policies that manage the secure configuration and patching of their ICT systems are subject to the following risks:

Unauthorised changes to systems An attacker could make unauthorised changes to ICT systems or information, compromising confidentiality, availability and integrity

Exploitation of unpatched vulnerabilities New patches are released almost daily and the timely application of security patches is critical to preserving the confidentiality, integrity and availability of ICT systems. Attackers will attempt to exploit unpatched systems to provide them with unauthorised access to system resources and information. Many successful attacks are enabled by exploiting a vulnerability for which a patch had been issued prior to the attack taking place

Exploitation of insecure system configurations An attacker could exploit a system that has not been locked down or hardened by:

- Gaining unauthorised access to information assets or importing malware
- Exploiting unnecessary functionality that has not been removed or disabled to conduct
- attacks and gain unauthorised access to systems, services, resources and information
- Connecting unauthorised equipment to exfiltrate information or introduce malware
- Creating a back door to use in the future for malicious purposes

Increases in the number of security incidents Without an awareness of vulnerabilities that have been identified and the availability (or not) of patches and fixes, the business will be increasingly disrupted by security incidents

How can the risk be managed?

Develop corporate policies to update and patch systems
Use the latest versions of operating systems, web browsers and applications. Develop and implement corporate policies to ensure that security patches are applied in a timeframe that is commensurate with the organisation's overall risk management approach. Organisations should use automated patch management and software update tools.

Create and maintain hardware and software inventories
Create inventories of the authorised hardware and software that constitute ICT systems across the organisation. Ideally, suitably configured automated tools should be used to capture the physical location, the business owner and the purpose of the hardware together with the version and patching status of all software used on the system. The tools should also be used to identify any unauthorised hardware or software, which should be removed.

Lock down operating systems and software

Consider the balance between system usability and security and then document and implement a secure baseline build for all ICT systems, covering clients, mobile devices, servers, operating systems, applications and network devices such as firewalls and routers. Essentially, any services, functionality or applications that are not required to support the business should be removed or disabled. The secure build profile should be managed by the configuration control and management process and any deviation from the standard build should be documented and formally approved.

Conduct regular vulnerability scans
Organisations should run automated vulnerability scanning tools against all networked devices regularly and remedy any identified vulnerabilities within an agreed time frame. Organisations should also maintain their situational awareness of the threats and vulnerabilities they face.

Establish configuration control and management
Produce policies and procedures that define and support the configuration control and change management requirements for all ICT systems, including software.

Disable unnecessary input/output devices and removable media access
Assess business requirements for user access to input/output devices and removable media (this could include MP3 players and Smart phones). Disable ports and system functionality that is not needed by the business (which may include USB ports, CD/DVD/Card media drives)

Implement whitelisting and execution control
Create and maintain a whitelist of authorised applications and software that can be executed on ICT systems. In addition, ICT systems need to be capable of preventing the installation and execution of unauthorised software and applications by employing process execution controls, software application arbiters and only accepting code that is signed by trusted suppliers;

Limit user ability to change configuration
Provide users with the minimum system rights and permissions that they need to fulfil their business role. Users with 'normal' privileges

should be prevented from installing or disabling any software or services running on the system.

10 Steps to Cyber Security:
Step 3 - Network Security
Detailed cyber security information and advice concerning your organisation's network security.

Summary

Connecting to untrusted networks (such as the Internet) exposes corporate networks to attacks that seek to compromise the confidentiality, integrity and availability of Information and Communications Technologies (ICT) and the information they store and process. This can be prevented by developing policies and risk management approaches to protect corporate networks by applying security controls that are commensurate with the risks that have been identified and the organisation's risk appetite.

What is the risk?

Corporate networks need to be protected against both internal and external threats. The level to which networks are protected should be considered in the context of the organisation's risk appetite, risk assessment and corporate security policies.
Businesses that fail to protect their networks appropriately could be subject to a number of risks, including:

Leakage of sensitive corporate information Poor network design could be exploited by both internal and external attackers to compromise information or conduct unauthorised releases of sensitive information resulting in compromises in confidentiality, integrity and availability

Import and export of malware Failure to put in place appropriate boundary security controls could lead to the import of malware and the compromise of business systems. In addition, users could deliberately or accidentally release malware or other malicious content to business partners or the general public via network connections that are poorly designed and managed

Denial of service Networks that are connected to untrusted networks (such as the Internet) are vulnerable to denial of services attacks, where access to services and information is denied to legitimate users, compromising the availability of the system or service

Exploitation of vulnerable systems Attackers will exploit poorly protected networks to gain unauthorised access to compromise the confidentiality, integrity and availability of systems, services and information

Damage or defacement of corporate resources Attackers that have successfully compromised the network can damage internal and externally facing systems and information (such as defacing corporate websites), harming the organisation's reputation and customer confidence

How can the risk be managed?

Produce, implement and maintain network security policies that align with the organisation's broader information risk management policies and objectives. Follow recognised network design principles (i.e. ISO/IEC 27033-1:2009) to help define the necessary security qualities for the perimeter and internal network segments and ensure that all network devices are configured to the secure baseline build.

Police the network perimeter

Limit access to network ports, protocols and applications filtering and inspecting all traffic at the network perimeter to ensure that only traffic which is required to support the business is being exchanged. Control and manage all inbound and outbound network connections and deploy technical controls to scan for malware and other malicious content.

Install firewalls
Firewalls should be deployed to form a buffer zone between the untrusted external network and the internal network used by the business. The firewall rule set should deny traffic by default and a whitelist should be applied that only allows authorised protocols, ports and applications to communicate with authorised networks and network addresses. This will reduce the exposure of ICT systems to network based attacks.

Prevent malicious content
Deploy antivirus and malware checking solutions to examine both inbound and outbound data at the perimeter in addition to antivirus and malware protection deployed on internal networks and on host systems. The antivirus and malware solutions used at the perimeter should be different to those used to protect internal networks and systems in order to provide some additional defence in depth.

Protect the internal network
Ensure that there is no direct network connectivity between internal systems and systems hosted on untrusted networks (such as the Internet), limit the exposure of sensitive information and monitor network traffic to detect and react to attempted and actual network intrusions.

Segregate network as sets
Identify, group and isolate critical business information assets and services and apply appropriate network security controls to them.

Secure wireless devices
Wireless devices should only be allowed to connect to trusted wireless networks. All wireless access points should be secured. Security scanning tools should have the ability to detect and locate unauthorised wireless access points.

Protect internal Internet Protocol (IP) addresses
Implement capabilities (such as Network Address Translation) to prevent internal IP addresses from being exposed to external networks and attackers and ensure that it is not possible to route network traffic directly from untrusted networks to internal networks.

Enable secure administration
Administrator access to any network component should only be carried out over dedicated network infrastructure and secure channels using communication protocols that support encryption.

Configure the exception handling processes
Ensure that error messages returned to internal or external systems or users do not include sensitive information that may be useful to attackers.

Monitor the network

Tools such as network intrusion detection and network intrusion prevention should be placed on the network and configured by qualified staff to monitor traffic for unusual or malicious incoming and outgoing activity that could be indicative of an attack or an attempt. Alerts generated by the system should be promptly managed by appropriately trained staff.

Assurance processes

Conduct regular penetration tests of the network infrastructure and undertake simulated cyber attack exercises to ensure that all security controls have been implemented correctly and are providing the necessary levels of security.

10 Steps to Cyber Security:
Step 4 - Managing User Privileges

Detailed cyber security information and advice concerning how to manage user privileges within your organisation.

Summary

It is good practice for an organisation to manage the access privileges that users have to an Information and Communications Technologies (ICT), the information it holds and the services it provides. All users of ICT systems should only be provided with the privileges that they need to do their job. This principle is often referred to as 'Least Privilege'. A failure to manage user privileges appropriately may result in an increase in the number of deliberate and accidental attacks.

What is the risk?

Businesses and organisations should understand what access employees need to information, services and resources in order to do their job. Otherwise they will not be able to grant ICT system rights and permissions to individual users or groups of users that are proportionate to their role within the organisation. Failure to effectively manage user privileges could result in the following risks being realised:

Misuse of privileges Authorised users can misuse the privileges assigned to them to either deliberately or accidentally compromise ICT systems. For example to make unauthorised changes to the configuration of systems, leading to a loss of the confidentiality, integrity or availability of information or ICT systems

Increased attacker capability Attackers will use unused or compromised user accounts to carry out their attacks and, if allowed to, they will return and reuse the compromised account on numerous occasions, or sell the access to others. The system privileges provided to the original user of the compromised account will be available to the attacker to use. Ultimately attackers will seek to gain access to root or administrative accounts to allow them full access to all system information, services and resources

Negating established security controls Where attackers have privileged access to ICT systems they will attempt to cover their tracks by making changes to security controls or deleting accounting and audit logs so that their activities are not detected

How can the risk be managed?

Set up a personnel screening process
All users need to undergo some form of pre-employment screening to a level that is commensurate with the sensitivity of the information they will have access to.

Establish effective account management processes
Corporate processes and procedures should manage and review user accounts from creation and modification through to eventual deletion when a member of staff leaves. Unused or dormant accounts, perhaps provided for temporary staff or for testing purposes, should be removed or suspended in-line with corporate policy.

Establish policy and standards for user identification and access control
The quality of user passwords and their lifecycle should be determined by a corporate policy. Ideally they should be machine generated, randomised passwords. If this is not possible, password complexity rules should be enforced by the system. For some ICT systems an additional authentication factor (such as a physical token) may be necessary and this should be identified in the risk assessment. Access controls should be allocated on the basis of business need and 'Least Privilege'.

Limit user privileges
Users should only be provided with the rights and permissions to systems, services, information and resources that they need to fulfil their business role.

Limit the number and use of privileged accounts
Strictly control the number of privileged accounts for roles such as system or database administrators. Ensure that this type of account is not used for high risk or day to day user activities, for example to gain access to external email or browse the Internet. Provide administrators with normal accounts for business use. The

requirement to hold a privileged account should be reviewed more frequently than 'standard user' accounts.

Monitor all users
Monitor user activity, particularly all access to sensitive information and the use of privileged account actions, such as the creation of new user accounts, changes to user passwords or the deletion of accounts and audit logs.

Limit access to the audit system and the system activity logs
Activity logs from network devices should be sent to a dedicated accounting and audit system that is separated from the core network. Access to the audit system and the logs should be strictly controlled to preserve the integrity and availability of the content and all privileged user access recorded.

Educate users and maintain their awareness
Without exception, all users should be aware of the policy regarding acceptable account usage and their personal responsibility to adhere to corporate security policies and the disciplinary measures that could be applied for failure to do so.

10 Steps to Cyber Security:
Step 5 - User Education and Awareness

Detailed cyber security information and advice concerning user education and awareness within your organisation.

Summary

Unfortunately the use made by employees of an organisation's Information and Communications Technologies (ICT) brings with it various risks. It is critical for all staff to be aware of their personal security responsibilities and the requirement to comply with corporate security policies. This can be achieved through systematic delivery of a security training and awareness programme that actively seeks to increase the levels of security expertise and knowledge across the organisation as well as a security-conscious culture.

What is the risk?

Organisations that do not produce user security policies or train their users in recognised good security practices will be vulnerable to many of the following risks:

Unacceptable use Without a clear policy on what is considered to be acceptable; certain actions by users may contravene good security practice and could lead to the compromise of personal or sensitive commercial information that could result in legal or regulatory sanctions and reputational damage

Removable media and personally owned devices Unless it is clearly set out in policy and regularly communicated, staff may consider it acceptable to use their own removable media or connect their personal devices to the corporate infrastructure. This could potentially lead to the import of malware and the compromise of personal or sensitive commercial information

Legal and regulatory sanction If users are not aware of any special handling or the reporting requirements for particular classes of sensitive information the organisation may be subject to legal and regulatory sanctions

Incident reporting If users do not report incidents promptly the impact of any incident could be compounded

Security Operating Procedures If users are not trained in the secure use of their organisation's ICT systems or the functions of a security control, they may accidentally misuse the system, potentially compromising a security control and the confidentiality, integrity and availability of the information held on the system

External attack Users remain the weakest link in the security chain and they will always be a primary focus for a range of attacks (phishing, social engineering, etc) because, when compared to a technical attack, there is a greater likelihood of success and the attacks are cheaper to mount. In many instances, a successful attack only requires one user to divulge a logon credential or open an email with malicious content

Insider threat A significant change in an employee's personal situation could make them vulnerable to coercion and they may release personal or sensitive commercial information to others. Dissatisfied users may try to abuse their system level privileges or coerce other users, to gain access to information or systems to which they are not authorised. Equally, they may attempt to steal or physically deface computer resources

How can the risk be managed?

Produce a user security policy
The organisation should develop and produce a user security policy (as part of their overarching corporate security policy) that covers acceptable use. Security procedures for all ICT systems should be produced that are appropriate and relevant to all business roles and processes.

Establish a staff induction process
New users (including contractors and third party users) should be made aware of their personal responsibility to comply with the corporate security policies as part of the induction process. The terms and conditions for their employment (contracts for contractors and third party users) must be formally acknowledged and retained to support any subsequent disciplinary action. Ideally, the initial user

registration process should also be linked to the organisation's technical access controls.

Maintain user awareness of the cyber risks faced by the organisation
Without exception, all users should receive regular refresher training on the cyber risks to the organisation and to them as both employees and individuals.

Support the formal assessment of Information Assurance (IA) skills
Staff in security roles should be encouraged to develop and formally validate their IA skills through enrolment on a recognised certification scheme for IA Professionals. Some security related roles such as system administrators, incident management team members and forensic investigators will require specialist training.

Monitor the effectiveness of security training
Establish mechanisms to test the effectiveness and value of the security training provided to all staff. This should be done through formal feedback and potentially by including questions in the staff survey on security training and the organisation's security culture. Those areas that regularly feature in security reports or achieve the lowest feedback ratings should be targeted for remedial action.

Promote an incident reporting culture
The organisation should enable a security culture that empowers staff to voice their concerns about poor security practices and security incidents to senior managers, without fear of recrimination.

Establish a formal disciplinary process
All staff should be made aware that any abuse of the organisation's security policies will result in disciplinary action being taken against them.

10 Steps to Cyber Security:
Step 6 - Incident Management
Detailed cyber security information and advice concerning incident management within your organisation.

Summary

All organisations will experience an information security incident at some point. Investment in establishing effective incident management policies and processes will help to improve resilience, support business continuity, improve customer and stakeholder confidence and reduce any financial impact.

What is the risk?

Security incidents are inevitable and they will vary in their business impact. All incidents need to be effectively managed, particularly those that invoke the organisation's disaster recovery and business continuity plans. Some incidents can, on further analysis, be indicative of more severe underlying problems. If businesses fail to implement an incident management capability that can detect, manage and analyse security incidents the following risks could be realised:

A major disruption of business operations Failure to realise that an incident has occurred and manage it effectively may compound the impact of the incident, leading to a long term outage, serious financial loss and erosion of customer confidence

Continual business disruption An organisation that fails to address the root cause of incidents by addressing weaknesses in the corporate security architecture could be exposed to consistent and damaging business disruption

Failure to comply with legal and regulatory reporting requirements An incident resulting in the compromise of sensitive information covered by mandatory reporting controls that are not adhered to could lead to legal or regulatory penalties. The organisation's business profile will determine the type and nature of incidents that may occur, and the impact they will have, and so a risk-based approach that considers all business processes should be used to shape the incident management plans. In addition, the quality and effectiveness of the security policies and the standards applied by the organisation will also be contributing factors to preventing incidents.

How can the risk be managed?

Obtain senior management approval and backing
The organisation's Board needs to understand the risks and benefits of incident management and provide appropriate funding to resource it and lead the delivery.

Establish an incident response capability
The organisation should identify the funding and resources to develop, deliver and maintain an organisation-wide incident management capability that can address the full range of incidents that could occur. This capability could be outsourced to a reputable supplier, such as those on the Cyber Incident Response (CIR) scheme. The supporting policy processes and plans should be risk based and cover any legal and regulatory reporting or data accountability requirements.

Provide specialist training
The incident response team may need specialist knowledge and expertise across a number of technical (including forensic investigation) and non-technical areas. The organisation should identify recognised sources of specialist incident management training and maintain the organisation's skill base.

Define the required roles and responsibilities
The organisation needs to appoint and empower specific individuals (or suppliers) to handle ICT incidents and provide them with clear terms of reference to manage any type of incident that may occur.

Establish a data recovery capability
Data losses occur and so a systematic approach to the backup of the corporate information asset base should be implemented. Backup media should be held in a physically secure location on-site and off-site where at all possible and the ability to recover archived data for operational use should be regularly tested.

Test the incident management plans

All plans supporting security incident management (including Disaster Recover and Business Continuity) should be regularly tested. The outcome of the tests should be used to inform the development and gauge the effectiveness of the incident management plans.

Decide what information will be shared and with whom

For information bound by specific legal and regulatory requirements the organisation may have to report any incidents that affect the status of that information within a specific timeframe. All internal and external reporting requirements should be clearly identified in the Incident Management Plans.

Collect and analyse post-incident evidence

The preservation and analysis of the user or network activity that led up to the event is critical to identify and remedy the root cause of an incident. The collected evidence could potentially support any follow on disciplinary or legal action and the incident management policy needs to set out clear guidelines to follow that comply with a recognised code of practice.

Conduct a lessons learned review

Log the actions taken during an incident and review the performance of the incident management process post incident (or following a test) to see what aspects worked well and what could be improved. Review the organisational response and update any related security policy, process or user training that could have prevented the incident from occurring.

Educate users and maintain their awareness

All users should be made aware of their responsibilities and the procedures they should follow to report and respond to an incident. Equally, all users should be encouraged to report any security weaknesses or incident as soon as possible and without fear of recrimination.

Report criminal incidents to Law Enforcement

It is important that online crimes are reported to Action Fraud or the relevant law enforcement agency to build a clearer view of the national threat picture and deliver an appropriate response.

10 Steps to Cyber Security:
Step 7 - Malware Prevention

Detailed cyber security information and advice concerning malware prevention within your organisation.

Summary

Any information exchange carries a degree of risk as it could expose the organisation to malicious code and content (malware) which could seriously damage the confidentiality, integrity and availability of the organisation's information and Information and Communications Technologies (ICT) on which it is hosted. The risk may be reduced by implementing security controls to manage the risks to all business activities.

What is the risk?

Malware infections can result in the disruption of business services, the unauthorised export of sensitive information, material financial loss and legal or regulatory sanctions. The range, volume and originators of information exchanged with the business and the technologies that support them provide a range of opportunities for malware to be imported. Examples include:

Email Still provides the primary path for internal and external information exchange. It can be used for targeted or random attacks (phishing) through malicious file attachments that will release their payload when the file is opened or contain embedded links that redirect the recipient to a website that then downloads malicious content

Web browsing and access to social media Uncontrolled browsing, including access to social media websites and applications, could provide an opportunity for an attacker to direct malicious content to a individual user or lead to the download of malicious content from a compromised or malicious website

Removable media and personally owned devices Malware can be transferred to a corporate ICT system through the use of removable media or the connection of a personally owned device

How can the risk be managed?

Develop and publish corporate policies
Develop and implement policies, standards and processes that deliver the overall risk management objectives but directly address the business processes that are vulnerable to malware.

Establish anti-malware defences across the organisation
Agree a top level corporate approach to managing the risk from malware that is applicable and relevant to all business areas.

Scan for malware across the organisation
Protect all host and client machines with antivirus solutions that will actively scan for malware.

Manage all data import and export
All information supplied to or from the organisation electronically should be scanned for malicious content.

Blacklist malicious websites
Ensure that the perimeter gateway uses blacklisting to block access to known malicious websites.

Provide dedicated media scanning machines
Standalone workstations (with no network connectivity) should be provided and equipped with two antivirus products. The workstation should be capable of scanning the content contained on any type of media and, ideally, every scan should be traceable to an individual.

Establish malware defences

Malware can attack any system process or function so the adoption of security architecture principles that provide multiple defensive layers (defence-in-depth) should be considered. The following controls are considered essential to manage the risks from malware:

Deploy antivirus and malicious code checking solutions with capabilities to continuously scan inbound and outbound objects at the perimeter, on internal networks and on host systems, preferably using different products at each layer. This will increase detection capabilities whilst reducing risks posed by any deficiencies in individual products. Any suspicious or infected objects should be quarantined for further analysis.

Deploy a content filtering capability on all external gateways to try to prevent attackers delivering malicious code to the common desktop applications used by the user, the web browser being a prime example. Content filtering can also help to counter the risks from a compromised information release mechanism or authorisation process that may allow sensitive data to be sent to external networks.

Install firewalls on the host and gateway devices and configure them to deny traffic by default, allowing only connectivity associated with known white listed applications

If the business processes can support it, disable scripting languages such as Windows

Scripting, Active X, VBScript and JavaScript. Where possible, disable the auto run function to prevent the automatic import of malicious code from any type of removable media. Equally, if removable media is introduced, the system should automatically scan it for malicious content Regularly scan every network component and apply security patches in compliance with the corporate security patching and vulnerability management policy

Apply the secure baseline build to every network device and mobile platform.

User education and awareness

Users should understand the risks from malware and the day to day secure processes they need to follow to prevent a malware infection from occurring. The security operating procedures for the corporate desktop should contain the following:

- Comply with the removable media policy at all times
- Do not open attachments from unsolicited emails
- Do not click on hyperlinks in unsolicited emails
- Do not connect any unapproved removable media or any unapproved personally owned device to the corporate network.

For more information consult the BYOD Guidance on www.gov.uk
Report any strange or unexpected system behaviours to the appropriate security team
Maintain an awareness of how to report a security incident

10 Steps to Cyber Security:
Step 8 - Monitoring
Detailed cyber security information and advice about monitoring your organisation's ICT activity.

Summary

Monitoring Information and Communications Technologies (ICT) activity allows businesses to better detect attacks and react to them appropriately whilst providing a basis upon which lessons can be learned to improve the overall security of the business. In addition, monitoring the use of ICT systems allows the business to ensure that systems are being used appropriately in accordance with organisational policies. Monitoring is often a key capability needed to comply with security, legal and regulatory requirements.

What is the risk?

Monitoring the organisation's ICT systems provides the business with the means to assess how they are being used by authorised users and if they have been or are being attacked. Without the ability to monitor, an organisation will not be able to:

Detect attacks Either originating from outside the organisation or attacks as a result of deliberate or accidental insider activity.

React to attacks So that an appropriate and proportionate response can be taken to prevent or minimise the resultant impact of an attack on the business.

Account for activity The business will not have a complete understanding of how their ICT systems or information assets are being used or enforce user accountability Failure to monitor ICT systems and their use for specific business processes could lead to non-compliance with the corporate security policy and legal or regulatory requirements or result in attacks going unnoticed.

How can the risk be managed?

Businesses need to put strategies, policies, systems and processes in place to ensure that they are capable of monitoring their ICT systems and respond appropriately to attacks. A consistent approach to monitoring needs to be adopted across the business that is based on a clear understanding of the risks.

Establish a monitoring strategy and supporting policies
Develop and implement an organisational monitoring strategy and policy based on an assessment of the risks. The strategy should take into account any previous security incidents and attacks and align with the organisation's incident management policies.

Monitor all ICT systems
Ensure that the solution monitors all networks and host systems (such as clients and servers) potentially through the use of Network and Host Intrusion Detection Systems (NIDS/HIDS) and Prevention Solutions (NIPS/HIPS), supplemented as required by Wireless Intrusion Detection Systems (WIDS). These solutions should provide both signature based capabilities to detect known attacks and heuristic capabilities to detect potentially unknown attacks through new or unusual system behaviour.

Monitor network traffic
The inbound and outbound network traffic traversing network boundaries should be continuously monitored to identify unusual activity or trends that could indicate attacks and the compromise of data. The transfer of sensitive information, particularly large data transfers or unauthorised encrypted traffic should automatically generate a security alert and prompt a follow up investigation. The analysis of network traffic can be a key tool in preventing the loss of data.

Monitor all user activity
The monitoring capability should have the ability to generate audit logs that are capable of identifying unauthorised or accidental input, misuse of technology or data. Critically, it should be able to identify the user, the activity that prompted the alert and the information they were attempting to access.

Test legal compliance

Ensure that the monitoring processes comply with legal or regulatory constraints on the monitoring of user activity.

Fine-tune monitoring systems

Ensure that monitoring systems are fine-tuned appropriately only to collect logs, events and alerts that are relevant in the context of delivering the requirements of the monitoring policy. Inappropriate collection of monitoring information could breach data protection and privacy legislation. It could also be costly in terms storing the audit information and could hinder the efficient detection of real attacks.

Establish a centralised collection and analysis capability

Develop and deploy a centralised capability that can collect and analyse accounting logs and security alerts from ICT systems across the organisation, including user systems, servers, network devices, and including security appliances, systems and applications. Much of this should be automated due to the volume of data involved enabling analysts to quickly identify and investigate anomalies. Ensure that the design and implementation of the centralised solution does not provide an opportunity for attackers to bypass normal network security and access controls.

Ensure there is sufficient storage

Security managers should determine the types of information needed to satisfy the organisation's monitoring policy. Vast quantities of data can be generated and appropriate storage will need to be made available. The organisation will also need to consider the sensitivity of the processed audit logs and any requirement for archiving to satisfy any regulatory or legal requirements.

Provide resilient and synchronised timing

Ensure that the monitoring and analysis of audit logs is supported by a centralised and synchronised timing source that is used across the entire organisation to time-stamp audit logs, alerts and events to support incident response, security investigations and disciplinary or legal action.

Train the security personnel

Ensure that security personnel receive appropriate training on the deployment of monitoring capability and the analysis of security alerts, events and accounting logs.

Align the incident management policies
Ensure that policies and processes are in place to appropriately manage and respond to incidents detected by monitoring solutions.

Conduct a lessons learned review
Ensure that processes are in place to test monitoring capabilities and learn from security incidents and improve the efficiency of the monitoring capability.

10 Steps to Cyber Security:
Step 9 - Removable Media Controls
Detailed cyber security information and advice concerning your organisation's removable media controls.

Summary

Failure to control or manage the use of removable media can lead to material financial loss, the theft of information, the introduction of malware and the erosion of business reputation. It is good practice to carry out a risk benefit analysis of the use of removable media and apply appropriate and proportionate security controls, in the context of their business and risk appetite.

What is the risk?

The use of removable media to store or transfer significant amounts of personal and commercially sensitive information is an everyday business process. However, if organisations fail to control and manage the import and export of information from their Information and Communications Technologies (ICT) using removable media they could be exposed to the following risks:

Loss of information The physical design of removable media can result in it being misplaced or stolen, potentially compromising the confidentiality and availability of the information stored on it

Introduction of malware The uncontrolled use of removable media will increase the risk from malware if the media can be used on multiple ICT systems

Information leakage Some media types retain information after user deletion; this could lead to an unauthorised transfer of information between systems

Reputational damage A loss of sensitive data often attracts media attention which could erode customer confidence in the business

Financial loss If sensitive information is lost or compromised the organisation could be subjected to financial penalties

How can the risk be managed?

Removable media should only be used to store or transfer information as a last resort, under normal circumstances information should be stored on corporate systems and exchanged using appropriately protected and approved information exchange connections.

Produce corporate policies
Develop and implement policies, processes and solutions to control the use of removable media for the import and export of information.

Limit the use of removable media
Where the use of removable media is unavoidable the business should limit the media types that can be used together with the users, systems and types of information that can be stored or transferred on removable media.

Scan all media for malware
Protect all host systems (clients and servers) with an anti-virus solution that will actively scan for malware when any type of removable media is introduced. The removable media policy should also ensure that any media brought into the organisation is scanned for malicious content by a standalone media scanner before any data transfer takes place.

Audit media holdings regularly
All removable media should be formally issued by the organisation to individuals who will be accountable for its secure use and return for destruction or reuse. Records of holdings and use should be made available for audit purposes.

Encrypt the information held on the media
Where removable media has to be used, the information should be encrypted. The type of encryption should be proportionate to the value of the information and the risks posed to it.

Lock down access to media drives

The secure baseline build should deny access to media drives (including USB drives) by default and only allow access to approved authorised devices.

Monitor systems
The monitoring strategy should include the capability to detect and react to the unauthorised use of removable media within an acceptable time frame.

Actively manage the reuse and disposal of removable media
Where removable media is to be reused or destroyed then appropriate steps should be taken to ensure that previously stored information will not be accessible. The processes will be dependent on the value of the information and the risks posed to it and could range from an approved overwriting process to the physical destruction of the media by an approved third party.

Educate users and maintain their awareness
Ensure that all users are aware of the risks posed to the organisation from the use of removable media and their personal security responsibility for following the corporate removable media security policy.

10 Steps to Cyber Security:
Step 10 - Home and Mobile Working
Detailed cyber security information and advice concerning home and mobile working.

Summary

Mobile working offers great business benefit but exposes the organisation to risks that will be challenging to manage. Mobile working extends the corporate security boundary to the user's location. It is advisable for organisations to establish risk-based policies and procedures that cover all types of mobile devices and flexible working if they are to effectively manage the risks. Organisations should also plan for an increase in the number of security incidents and have a strategy in place to manage the loss or compromise of personal and commercially sensitive information and any legal, regulatory or reputational impact that may result.

What is the risk?

Mobile working entails the transit and storage of information assets outside the secure corporate infrastructure, probably across the Internet to devices that may have limited security features. Mobile devices are used in public spaces where there is the risk of oversight and they are also highly vulnerable to theft and loss. If the organisation does not follow good practice security principles and security policies the following risks could be realised:

Loss or theft of the device Mobile devices are highly vulnerable to being lost or stolen because they are attractive and valuable devices. They are often used in open view in locations that cannot offer the same level of physical security as the organisation's own premises.

Being overlooked Some users will have to work in public open spaces where they are vulnerable to being observed when working on their mobile device, potentially compromising personal or sensitive commercial information or their user credentials.

Loss of credentials If user credentials (such as username, password, token) are stored with a device used for remote working and it is lost or stolen, the attacker could potentially compromise the confidentiality, integrity and availability of the organisation's Information and Communications Technologies (ICT).

Tampering An attacker may attempt to subvert the security controls on the device through the insertion of malicious software or hardware if the device is left unattended. This may allow them to monitor all user activity on the mobile device that could result in the compromise of the confidentiality or integrity of the information.

Compromise of the secure configuration Without correct training a user may accidentally or intentionally remove or reconfigure a security enforcing control on the mobile device and compromise the secure configuration. This could expose the device to a range of logical attacks that could result in the compromise or loss of any personal or sensitive commercial information the device is storing

How can the risk be managed?

Assess the risks and create a mobile working security policy

Assess the risks to all types of mobile working (including remote working where the device connects to the corporate network infrastructure). The resulting mobile security policy should determine aspects such as the processes for authorising users to work offsite, device acquisition and support, the type of information that can be stored on devices and the minimum procedural security controls. The risks to the corporate network from mobile devices should be assessed and consideration given to an increased level of monitoring on all remote connections and the corporate systems being accessed.

Educate users and maintain their awareness
Without exception, all users should be trained on the secure use of their mobile device for the locations they will be working in. Users should be capable of operating the device securely by following their user specific security procedures at all times, which should as a minimum include direction on: secure storage and management of their user credentials incident reporting environmental awareness (the risks from being overlooked, etc.)

Apply the secure baseline build
All ICT systems should be configured to the secure baseline build including all types of mobile device used by the organisation.

Consider integrating the security controls provided in the End User Device guidance (available on www.gov.uk) into the baseline build for mobile devices.

Protect data at rest

Minimise the amount of information stored on a mobile device to only that which is needed to fulfil the business activity that is being delivered when working outside the normal office environment. If the device supports it, encrypt the data at rest.

Protect data in transit

If the user is working remotely the connection back to the corporate network will probably use an untrusted public network such as the Internet. The device and the information exchange should be protected by an appropriately configured Virtual Private Network (VPN).

Review the corporate incident management plans

Mobile working attracts significant risks and security incidents will occur even when users follow the security procedures (such as a forced attack where the user is physically attacked to gain control of the device). The corporate incident management plans should be sufficiently flexible to deal with the range of security incidents that could occur, including the loss or compromise of a device in international locations. Ideally, technical processes should be in place to remotely disable a device that has been lost or at least deny it access to the corporate network.

Here are the 10 steps repeated showing where ASW failed to follow good practice.

Step 1 - Information Risk Management Regime

Detailed cyber security information and advice concerning your organisation's information risk management regime.

How can the risk be managed?

Establish a governance framework

> *The IT department was too busy working to their own agenda. It probably didn't suite them to have more visibility*

Determine the organisation's risk appetite

> *There is no evidence that IT had ever gone to the Board with a risk profile. For their part the Directors seemed to be content to leave IT alone, just so long as they kept the systems running.*

Maintain the Board's engagement with information risk

> *There was no engagement with the Board.*

Produce supporting policies

> *IT completely failed to produce any policies, so the users didn't know what was expected of them.*

Adopt a lifecycle approach to information risk management

> *IT within ASW had no engagement with the Board and therefore never had to justify their role*

Apply recognised standards

> *Because IT was remote from the business, they were working to their own standards. The Board seemed happy to leave them alone. This can be a risk with senior managers not wanting to get involved in a technical area that they don't understand*

Make use of endorsed assurance schemes

> *If IT had worked to the Cyber Essentials Scheme, then many of their problems would have been identified earlier.*

Educate users and maintain their awareness

Security is not common sense, it has to be taught. IT had a responsibility to educate the users in order to protect the systems and eventually, the business

Promote a risk management culture

There was probably a fault with the audit regime that didn't ensure that IT was engaging with the business.

Step 2 - Secure Configuration

Detailed cyber security information and advice concerning the secure configuration of your organisation.

How can the risk be managed?

Develop corporate policies to update and patch systems

Policies are vital to the smooth running to the company systems.

Create and maintain hardware and software inventories

When asked for an inventory of the hardware and software, IT couldn't provide one. This is a bad weakness and something that the Auditors should have identified.

Lock down operating systems and software

This is a vital control. By leaving the operating system open a hacker or a virus may be able to replace code that you are not using with code of their own.

Conduct regular vulnerability scans

Vulnerability scans are not the same as a full penetration test, they are very much cheaper to run but will identify missing patches that may leave you vulnerable to attack. Automated scans may be purchased very reasonably

Establish configuration control and management

This is an important part of running an IT department if it is to provide a good service to a company. ASW failed to have this in place.

Disable unnecessary input/output devices and removable media access

Many companies fail to control their removable media and to prevent media from executing automatically. This has been a popular way of introducing viruses into company networks.

Implement whitelisting and execution control

There are a number of whitelisting solutions on the market and some are more technical than others. If you are looking for it is worth spending some time researching what is available.

Limit user ability to change configuration

This is one thing that ASW seems to have done correctly. There is evidence that their IT team had control of what was installed, but not in a formal way.

Step 3 - Network Security

Detailed cyber security information and advice concerning your organisation's network security.

How can the risk be managed?

Police the network perimeter

The limiting of access to network ports and services is part of the hardening process. This had not been undertaken

Install firewalls

Firewalls had been installed but not correctly monitored. Any changes to the Firewall configuration should be checked on a regular basis.

Prevent malicious content

The systems seem to have been protected by antivirus (as Laura didn't comment on this).

Protect the internal network

ASW had tried to build a separate network that contained the sensitive internal elements but a lack of control and monitoring meant that the controls were being bypassed.

Segregate network as sets

IT thought this had been achieved but failed to monitor

Secure wireless devices

> *The use of wireless devices doesn't seem to have been a problem as Laura didn't highlight this in his findings*

Protect internal Internet Protocol (IP) addresses

> *The IT team at ASW thought that they had segregated the sensitive data from the web-site.*

Enable secure administration

> *While the IT team had separated the live data from their web-site they still used a single network for administering the system. There is no evidence that they used a separate logon to access the business servers.*

Configure the exception handling processes

> *All error handling seems to have been restricted to waiting for IDS or Firewall alerts. When Steve leaves to get his new car, he asks Anne, who is a developer, to monitor the network perimeter.*

Monitor the network

> *The network had a Firewall (or Firewall pairs, this isn't clear) and an IDS. These were not actively monitored, since the change of configuration wasn't seen*

Assurance processes

> *No penetration tests had been conducted. These should have listed the privileged accounts and the change of Firewall configuration*

Step 4 - Managing User Privileges

Detailed cyber security information and advice concerning how to manage user privileges within you organisation.

How can the risk be managed?

Set up a personnel screening process

> *Given that ASW worked in PR and marketing there was sensitive intellectual property but not data that would fall under the City financial regulators. It is*

likely that the HR process relied on the interviewee being "known" to the management

Establish effective account management processes

We know that there were more accounts than there were staff, so it is likely that the accounts were kept on the system "just in case"

Establish policy and standards for user identification and access control

We know that the quality of passwords was poor. The system should have been forcing users to have complex passwords (say 3 of the following upper-case letters, lower-case letters, numbers and special characters)

Limit user privileges

There does seem to be a limit to the authority of the general users

Limit the number and use of privileged accounts

There were not many privileged accounts, though it is likely that anyone in IT would be given Admin rights.

Monitor all users

User monitoring does not seem to be in place, since the additional administrator accounts hadn't been seen

Limit access to the audit system and the system activity logs

Access to the audit files was controlled by simply not having any! This would hamper any investigation.

Educate users and maintain their awareness

There doesn't seem to have been any user training or awareness. When the users are asked why they have done anything they say that they have just copied what they have seen.

Step 5 - User Education and Awareness

Detailed cyber security information and advice concerning user education and awareness within your organisation.

How can the risk be managed?

Produce a user security policy
> *The lack of a security policy indicates a wider lack of control*

Establish a staff induction process
> *We don't know if there is any form of induction, but it seems unlikely*

Maintain user awareness of the cyber risks faced by the organisation
> *We know from what happened within the e-mail system that user awareness is very poor*

Support the formal assessment of Information Assurance (IA) skills
> *IA does not seem to have been a priority. Given the size of the company it is unlikely that they would have a full-time IA person but the skills should be shared among the IT staff.*

Monitor the effectiveness of security training
> *There is no security training*

Promote an incident reporting culture
> *This would have helped promote awareness among the staff and management*

Establish a formal disciplinary process
> *With no policies and no awareness, a disciplinary process would be doomed before it started. ASW need to take the well being of the company and the staff more seriously*

Step 6 - Incident Management

Detailed cyber security information and advice concerning incident management within your organisation.

How can the risk be managed?

Obtain senior management approval and backing
> *Senior management is not aware of what IT is doing or what it could do for the company. This is a failure of IT and the Board*

Establish an incident response capability

It is possible that this incident could have been a wake-up call if it weren't for the fact that it is already too late

Provide specialist training

The need for training is very poor. In fact when Paul has been away to a training course or a seminar he has used that as an excuse to continue his affair. This shows how little regard he paid to training

Define the required roles and responsibilities

This is completely lacking. It is a mix of IT, senior management and HR

Establish a data recovery capability

Like all recovery processes it is essential that they are put in place and then tested. ASW have failed to even assess the need

Test the incident management plans

As above

Decide what information will be shared and with whom

ASW doesn't seem to have conducted any assessments, they are running blind and hoping for the best

Collect and analyse post-incident evidence

This would be impossible given the lack of audit records

Conduct a lessons learned review

There is no evidence that there is any understanding of the need for such a review

Educate users and maintain their awareness

If the users are not made aware of the need for security and resilience, then there will be no buy-in from them

Report criminal incidents to Law Enforcement

While the information that the criminals are after is intellectual property, in the form of the company accounts, there has been an offence under the Computer Misuse legislation. Laura would recommend that ASW report the crime but in this case it will be too late and the police will have little to go on

Step 7 - Malware Prevention

Detailed cyber security information and advice concerning malware prevention within your organisation.

How can the risk be managed?

Develop and publish corporate policies

> *There are no written policies to provide guidance to the staff of ASW. This helped cause a series of failings*

Establish anti-malware defences across the organisation

> *As this particular hack was caused by poor perimeter security and not checking their suppliers, the issue of Malware didn't arise but we do know that there was anti-virus on the PCs but a general sweep wasn't conducted at regular intervals as it should have been.*

Scan for malware across the organisation

> *See above*

Manage all data import and export

> *While the individual PCs had this capability, the lack of any policies meant that any scanning would only be performed if the users were aware of the need*

Blacklist malicious websites

> *Given the ease with which Malcolm had been viewing pornography, it suggests that there no restrictions on what a user could access*

Provide dedicated media scanning machines

> *This is a low-cost and very sensible option but ASW wouldn't have seen this as a priority*

Establish malware defences

> *Other than a basic anti-virus system on the computers, it seems that no thought had been given to how malicious code could work through their systems*

User education and awareness

> *There was no user education at all. Even though ASW was a small company, the lack of user training would have caused a problem sooner or later. As stated earlier, cyber security is not common sense, it has to be taught*

Step 8 - Monitoring

Detailed cyber security information and advice about monitoring your organisation's ICT activity.

How can the risk be managed?

Establish a monitoring strategy and supporting policies
> *There were no policy documents and therefore no strategies*

Monitor all ICT systems
> *Only the perimeter was monitored and then, just the Firewall and IDS*

Monitor network traffic
> *If the network had been monitored, then the busy e-mail server may have been noticed. This may have given them an early warning of the hack*

Monitor all user activity
> *The users were left to their own devices with little advice or guidance. The only time that the users seem to have been given any help was when Steve notices a problem. The users do not seem to have been in the habit of talking to IT*

Test legal compliance
> *Other than the audit, there is no evidence of anyone ensuring that they met their legal obligations*

Fine-tune monitoring systems
> *This had not been done*

Establish a centralised collection and analysis capability
> *The IT team were not collecting any audit data*

Ensure there is sufficient storage
> *This was not a consideration*

Provide resilient and synchronised timing
> *This was completely missing*

Train the security personnel
> *The lack of training is obvious*

Align the incident management policies
> *There were no policies*

Conduct a lessons learned review

They did try to do this but it was all too late to save the company

Step 9 - Removable Media Controls
Detailed cyber security information and advice concerning your organisation's removable media controls.

How can the risk be managed?

Produce corporate policies
> *The lack of corporate policies is not just an IT issue, the Board and the Auditors must share in the lack of oversight*

Limit the use of removable media
> *There seem to be no controls in place.*

Scan all media for malware
> *The lack of security awareness training and the means that this was only ever going to be patchy*

Audit media holdings regularly
> *Auditing as a whole has been neglected*

Encrypt the information held on the media
> *There is no evidence that any static encryption was undertaken*

Lock down access to media drives
> *There was no attempt to limit what the users could do*

Monitor systems
> *With the exception of the network perimeter, there seems to have been no monitoring*

Actively manage the reuse and disposal of removable media
> *While there seems to have been little use made of removable media, there is no evidence of any controls or guidance*

Educate users and maintain their awareness
> *User awareness was ignore by IT*

Step 10 - Home and Mobile Working

Detailed cyber security information and advice concerning home and mobile working.

How can the risk be managed?

Assess the risks and create a mobile working security policy

> *IT should have designed and implemented a secure remote working system. They seem to have provided the minimum to satisfy the users*

Educate users and maintain their awareness

> *There is no evidence of any user training and therefore no attempt at maintaining their awareness*

Apply the secure baseline build

> *Remote working is an area that can easily go wrong for companies. IT should be very active in providing guidance for the users*

Protect data at rest

> *If an ASW employee were to lose their personal device, it is very unlikely that IT would have been able to remotely wipe the device. This would have been a serious risk*

Protect data in transit

> *We have no information about the level of protection given to data in transit*

Review the corporate incident management plans

> *There seem to have been no incident plans*

Part 3

Where can you go for help?

Having given you a number of problems to think about, it is worth saying that you are not without help. There are many organisations and companies that you can go for help and advice. Below is a list of some companies and organisations that we have had experience of working with. We do not recommend any particular service because in order to do so we would need to understand exactly what you are trying to achieve and the precise nature of your business. However, this should be a good starting place for you to build your knowledge. This is not meant to be an exhaustive list but simply some examples of resources that we have used over the years. Of course, if you have a particular question, then using your favourite search engine should provide you with information.

Many of the organisations we have listed will be happy to talk to small companies and give them guidance.

Cyber Security.

Cyber Essentials – This is a government-backed cyber security certification scheme that sets out a baseline of cyber security suitable for all organisations. The scheme's five security controls can prevent "around 80% of cyber attacks" allowing you to focus instead on your core business objectives. By properly implementing cyber security controls, you will also drive business efficiency throughout the organisation, saving money and improving productivity.

A Cyber Essentials or Cyber Essentials Plus badge will enhance your business's reputation and open up new commercial opportunities by proving to your customers that you take the security of their information seriously and are taking the necessary steps to reduce cyber risks.

Go to - http://www.itgovernance.co.uk/cyber-essentials-scheme.aspx

Risk Register creation - One company that specialised in risk management is Acuity. They have specialist software that will help guide you through the generation and maintenance of a risk-register. See www.acuity.com

List of scanners and penetration testers.

Automated Scanning.

Penetration testing is simulating an attack from a hacker. Some testing companies will offer you the use of automated scanners, and these are the basic form of attack. A scanner will highlight a weakness in your security but will not automatically try to exploit it. Companies like those below offer a scanning service that is low cost and designed to be used by IT staff who can understand the brief explanations given in the reports.

Qualys – Is an automated scanner that will check your network for vulnerabilities. While this is not as thorough as a full penetration test conducted by a skilled consultant, it is thorough and generally represents good value for money. Their systems can operate to the PCI DSS standards.
www.qualys.com
Qualys also provide some useful free tools that are worth familiarising yourself with;
www.ssllabs.com will assess and score the strength of the HTTPS configuration of your website,
browsercheck.qualys.com will assess and score the security of your web browser, recommending updates for any common plug-ins.
www.qualys.com/forms/assetview is a free asset inventory tool to help you keep track of your hardware and software, which can quickly become a burden as your company grows.

Outpost24 – Is another automated scanning service provider that can assess your web presence, your internal networks, and fulfil PCI scanning requirements.
www.outpost24.com

Penetration testing.

Other penetration testers will conduct more sophisticated attacks and will use a variety of tools that the hackers will deploy. They may use a scanner but will go on to use a mix of **social engineering** tricks to try to fool your staff into giving out information and then exploit this. While this may seem a bit underhand, please remember that if a consultant can trick your staff into giving out information, then a skilled hacker will also succeed. The advantage of using a consultant to do it is the fact that they will then explain how they got the information and how an attacker would use it. These attacks can become very valuable lessons to train your staff. The thing to remember with social engineering is that it is normally conducted over the phone. If the staff member becomes suspicious, the attacker can simply hang-up and try another person later. The motto seems to be "Before you find your handsome Prince you have to kiss a lot of Frogs!"

ProCheckUp – ProCheckUp has a wealth of experience in Cyber Security consulting and specialise in manual and automated penetration testing. They have developed their own specialised knowledge based scanner that they use before confirming the results with manual checks. They operate to very high IT industry standards such as CREST, CESG, CHECK and PCI DSS. For more information see www.procheckup.com

NCC and **ContextIS** are both long established organisation with international reach and a diverse range of services in the information security world, each with membership of several select committees and response groups ensuring that they are able to accommodate any eventuality. Visit www.nccgroup.trust and www.contextis.com for further information.

Information Risk Management – IRM was founded in 1998 and have therefore been around for a long time in the Cyber Security world. They have offices in London and Cheltenham so that they can be close to their main customers. They offer some innovative solutions and operate to CREST, CESG, CHECK and PCI DSS standards. For more information visit www.irmplc.com

Physically penetrating your buildings.

The next level of attack comes from the companies who will try to gain physical access to your building. For most small companies this is a hard task because the staff working for you will tend to know all of the other employees. However, for a larger company, the ability to keep the bad guys out can be vital. Some of the most successful hacks in history started with a member of staff telling the attacker their user name and password. If an attacker can gain access to your building, they will be inside your IT network and can generally attach a device directly into your trusted (green) network zone. This is not an issue for most small companies but if you are holding very high value data, then you need to be aware of the tricks that the enemy will use.

First-Base – First Base is a well established company that uses a mixture of social engineering, physical penetration tests to try to gain access to your systems. They will also use "conventional" hacking tools. They are based in West Sussex on the south coast of England, but like all companies that operate in Cyber Space, can work anywhere the client requires. For more information visit www.firstbase.co.uk

Investigations.

So what do you do if you believe your systems have been attacked, or even hacked? The companies that perform penetration testing are generally able to assist with an investigation but there are other specialists. The following are companies you can call if you believe you have a problem or are at risk. They employ experienced investigators and can offer advice in confidence.

ESID Consulting – Is an independent specialist in all aspects of Internal / Workplace and Anti-Corruption Investigations, Information Security and Business Continuity. The company has specialist knowledge in carrying out employee investigations and digital forensics, where theft, misuse and "leakage" of corporate data and other sensitive information has occurred. They provide practical support and advice on securing your company data and protecting your business and clients' information. They achieve this through the creation and implementation of an appropriate Business Continuity Plan and Information Security Management System, or a review of your current arrangements www.esid.co.uk

Physical intrusion, investigations and corporate protection.

XIX Group – This is a specialist company that offers risk management solutions to corporate organisations and individuals. They are able to test your physical security, your disaster planning and train your staff in a variety of security related skills. If you have suffered a security breach, they can investigate and often help you to minimise the impact of the loss. Employing a number of Ex-Metropolitan Police specialists, they can often help companies regain control in what can be a fast moving incident. They will identify risks to high-profile people and conduct counter surveillance on high-risk companies and individuals. www.xixgroup.com

Your company reputation.

We looked at what your customers and employees think about your company and what they publish about you earlier in the book. It is wise to use a search engine to look for your company name as well as looking on any trade web-sites where reviews are published. If you use market-place companies like E-Bay or Amazon, then monitor your reputation and you should review sites like www.glassdoor.co.uk to see what your employees and ex-employees are saying.

Publications.

There are a number of publications that you can access over the Internet that will help you understand the various security threats and see what the latest attacks are.

The Register – is an online publication that looks at a number of IT topics, including security. To obtain a daily copy you will need to register but the publication is free. Go to www.theregister.co.uk for the main web-site or to account.theregister.co.uk to sign-up for your choice of topics.

SC Magazine – has a number of articles and reviews of Cyber Security products and well as explaining some of the key issues. www.scmagazineuk.com

Infosecurity Magazine – is another online magazine that offers news and comment to Cyber Security professionals. It is a good source of information. For more information go to www.infosecurity-magazine.com

Other Help

As with online publications, there are a number of organisations that will help with your Cyber Security needs.

US-CERT – is an American organisation and the initials stand for United States Computer Emergency Readiness Team. They offer a number of white-papers and articles about various aspects of Cyber Security and most of their publications are free. You can also subscribe to their alerting system by giving your e-mail address.

AV Systems.
Before investing in an anti-virus platform to help protect your systems and data you may want to review performance, keeping in mind that no AV tool will provide 100% protection and that the effectiveness of any tool

varies up or down over time. Two independent websites which conduct regular tests of AV effectiveness are www.av-test.org and www.av-comparatives.org

Microsoft Security Essentials comes as standard with any modern version of Windows
Symantec – www.symantec.com
Kaspersky – www.kaspersky.com
McCafee – www.mccafee.com

White-Lists.
White-Lists are simply a list of all programs and executables that may be used in your computer systems. If a program tries to run but is not on the list of approved programs, the system will not allow it to run. This gives a high degree of protection against rogue software that has been inserted into your systems but there is an overhead in administering the system.

Device Control
This is a way of controlling what external dev ices can be connected to a computer. This would limit a rogue user to connect a USB thumb drive to a computer port and then extract vast quantities of data. These systems will allow a very detailed amount of auditing of what has been extracted from your systems. There are a number of white-listing and device control systems but I have experience of using Lumension and found it to have many helpful features. Lumension Application and device control – www.lumension.com

Hard Disk Firewall (HDF).
This is a new approach to an old problem. Abatis is a security software development company that has created an innovative new Host Integrity Technology called HDF. HDF has been independently proven to stop malware from infecting servers, workstations, virtual devices, SCADA systems and mobile platforms. Available now for Linux and Microsoft platforms as old as Windows NT4 through to Windows 8.1, and soon: Google's Android. Lockheed Martin's evaluation confirmed not just the security capabilities and zero performance degradation, but also

quantified the energy saved by the protected device as equivalent to £35/$60 per server per annum. Forrester Research has identified HDF as a security technology that could dominate the future of anti-malware and Abatis as "A Company To Watch".
Abatis – www.abatis-HDF.com

Vendors.
Rather than setting up relationships with many various IT organisations for products and support it may be beneficial to get in touch with a vendor who can provide a one-stop-shop type of approach. Vendors are typically independent and have relationships with a variety of service providers so that they can tailor a solution to suit your specific needs, they often also have some consulting capabilities to help you get set up and some first line support capabilities for when things go wrong. While there are many vendors on the market you might want to take a look at ww.foursys.co.uk and www.nonstopit.com to get started.

The Police.
There are a number of specialist police units at a regional and a national level that you can turn to if you believe you have suffered a security breach. For serious organised crime fighting see the National Crime Agency www.nationalcrimeagency.gov.uk

Action Fraud is a specialist police unit that is there to help victims of fraud.
www.actionfraud.police.uk

Regulators and supporting organisations.

PCI – Payment Card Industry www.pcisecuritystandards.org
ICO – The Information Commissioner's Office www.ico.org.uk
SANS Institute www.sans.org
OWASP – Open Web Application Security Project www.owasp.org
Your Member of Parliament and MEP (or **MSP** in Scotland) for the UK

Organisations that will help small businesses.

Cyber Security Clusters – There are a number of Cyber Security Clusters around the UK and these are aimed at helping small businesses working in the Cyber Security sector. However, the various members of your local cluster may well provide a good source of help and advice on your IT Security issues. www.ukcybersecurityforum.com

The Federation of Small Businesses – Is an organisation that is designed to help small businesses. They can give advice and guidance to small businesses on a variety of matters. www.fsb.org.uk

British Computer Society – Is the Chartered Institute for IT. It has a number of local branches and specialist sections and is a good starting point for increasing your IT skills. The branch meetings and presentations are generally open to members and non-members alike, so it can be a good source of information and assistance. www.bcs.org.uk

Government – The government has a **Minister for small business, industry and enterprise.** https://www.gov.uk/government/ministers/minister-of-state-business-and-enterprise

Have I Been Pwned – Is a free subscription/notification website that will alert you if your email address (or any email address on your business domain) is exposed in a public data breach such as that which affected Adobe or Ashley Madison. Getting ahead of the curve can help you to take preventative or recovery measures before any damage is done, such as resetting passwords for the exposed accounts. www.haveibeenpwned.com *(The term Pwned came about because of a typing error in a games review where the author meant to type "owned" and wrote "pwned" instead, the term stuck)*

There are also a number of Government publications aimed at assisting small businesses with their Cyber security. Please see Part 2 for the "Government 10 steps to cyber security".

Check your favourite Internet search engine for the latest news and advice.